Presents

Master Blues Guitar
A Complete Course

Written & Method By
John McCarthy

Adapted By: Jimmy Rutkowski
Supervising Editor: John McCarthy
Music Transcribing & Engraving: Jimmy Rutkowski
Production Manager: John McCarthy
Layout, Graphics & Design: Jimmy Rutkowski
Photography: Rodney Dabney
Copy Editors: Cathy McCarthy

Cover Art Direction & Design:
Jimmy Rutkowski

HL217080
ISBN: 978-1-4950-8837-7
Produced by John McCarthy®
© 2017 McCarthy Publishing, LLC All Rights Reserved

Table of Contents

About the Author 4
Introduction 5
Icon Key 6

Beginner

Parts of the Guitar 7
Holding the Guitar 9
Essential Blues Tools 12
Tuning 13
Reading Chord Charts 14
Open Blues Chords 15
Open Chord Blues 18
Reading Tab 20
Basic Blues Rhythm 21
The Blues Shuffle 22
Reading a Scale Diagram 23
Minor Pentatonic Scales - Key of "A" 24
Lead Patterns 26
Bends 28
Hammer ons 30
Pull offs 30
Full Blues Lead 31
Creating a Great Blues Sound 32
Blues Riffs That Will Make Yo' Mama Scream! 33
Shuffle Blues Rhythm 34
Complete Blues Lead 35

Intermediate

Blues Scales - Key of "E" 37
Open String Blues Rhythm in "E" 39
Blues Lead in "E" 40
Bar Chords 41
12 Bar Blues Progression 44
12 Bar Theory 44
Skipping Strings - 3rds & 5ths 46
Blues Single Note Riff Rhythm 47
Slides & Vibrato 48
Rockin' The Blues Using Dead Strums 49
Blues Riffs That Will Make Yo' Mama Scream - Part 2 50
The B.B. Box 51
Open Chord Blues Smokin' Rhythm 52

Advanced Bonus Lessons

Major Pentatonic Scales - Key of "C" 54
"C" Fast Blues 56
The Talk Back Effect - Combining Major & Minor Scales 57
Improvisational Exercise 58
Advanced Bending Techniques 59
Bar Chord Review 60
Blues Techniques - Rakes 61
Blues Riffs That Will Make Yo' Mama Scream - Part 3 61
Advanced Jazz/Blues Chords 62
The Jazz/Blues Fuze - Complete Rhythm Progression 63
Triplet & Sixteenth Scale Patterns 64
Minor Pentatonic Scale Theory 65
Blues/Rock Rhythm 66
Classic Old School Blues Rhythm & Lead Combo 67
Still Getting the Blues - Circle of Fourths 68
Modern Blues Leads - Natural Minor Scales 69
Slide Techniques 70
Blues Rhythms 71

Appendix
Blues Word Search 74
Changing Your Strings 75
Practice Tips 76
Minor Pentatonic Scales: A Minor 77
Major Pentatonic Scales: A Major 78
Blues Scales: A Blues 79
Common Blues Progression Variations 80
Blues Chord Glossary 86
Blank Chord Paper 105
Blank Tab Paper 106
Blank Neck Paper 107
Blues Word Search Answer Key 108

Digital eBook

When you register this product at the Lesson Support site RockHouseMethod.com, you will receive a digital version of this book. This interactive eBook can be used on all devices that support Adobe PDF. This will allow you to access your book using the latest portable technology any time you want.

Introduction

Welcome to **The Rock House Method**® system of learning. You are joining millions of aspiring musicians around the world who use our easy-to-understand methods for learning to play music. Unlike conventional learning programs, **The Rock House Method**® is a four-part teaching system that employs DVD lesson video, downloadable backing tracks and 24/7 online lesson support along with this book to give you a variety of sources to assure a complete learning experience. The products can be used individually or together. The DVD that comes with this book matches the curriculum exactly, providing you with a live instructor for visual reference.

How to Use the Lesson Support Site

Every Rock House product offers FREE membership to our interactive *Lesson Support* site. Use the member number below to register at RockHouseMethod.com. Once registered, you can use this fully interactive site along with your product to enhance your learning experience, expand your knowledge, link with instructors, and connect with a community of people around the world who are learning to play music using **The Rock House Method**®. There are sections that directly correspond to this product within the *Additional Information* and *Backing Tracks* sections. There are also a variety of other tools you can utilize such as *Ask The Teacher*, *Quizzes*, *Reference Material*, *Definitions*, *Forums*, *Live Chats*, *Guitar Professor* and much more.

GO TO **ROCKHOUSEMETHOD.COM** AND REGISTER FOR LESSON SUPPORT

MEMBER NUMBER: BG883334

Icon Key

Throughout this book, you'll periodically notice the icons listed below. They indicate when there are additional learning tools available on our support website for the section you're working on. When you see an icon in the book, visit the member section of RockHouseMethod.com for musical backing tracks, additional information and learning utilities.

Backing Track

Many of the exercises in this book are intended to be played along with bass and drum rhythm tracks. This icon indicates that there is a backing track available for download on the *Lesson Support* site.

Additional Information

The question mark icon indicates there is more information for that section available on the *Lesson Support* site. It can be theory, more playing examples or tips.

Metronome

Metronome icons are placed next to the examples that we recommend you practice using a metronome. You can download a free, adjustable metronome from our *Lesson Support* site.

Tuner

Also found on the website is a free online tuner that you can use to help tune your instrument. You can download the free online tuner from RockHouseMethod.com.

Blues

Beginner

Parts of The Guitar

The guitar is divided into three main sections: the body, the neck and the headstock. The guitar's input jack will be located on the side or front of the body. The assembly that anchors the strings to the body is called the bridge. The saddles hold the strings properly in place; the height of each string (or action) can be adjusted with the saddle. Mounted to the body behind the strings are the pickups. A pickup functions like the guitar's microphone; it picks up the vibrations of the strings and converts them to a signal that travels through the guitar cord to the amplifier. Also located on the front of the body are the volume and tone knobs and the pickup selector switch or toggle switch. Strap buttons are located on both sides of the body where a guitar strap can be attached. The front face of the neck is called the fretboard (or fingerboard). The metal bars going across the fretboard are called frets. The dots are position markers (or fret markers) for visual reference to help you gauge where you are on the neck while playing. The nut is the string guide that holds the strings in place where the neck meets the headstock. The headstock contains the machine heads (also referred to as tuners); the machine heads are used to tune the strings by tightening or loosening them.

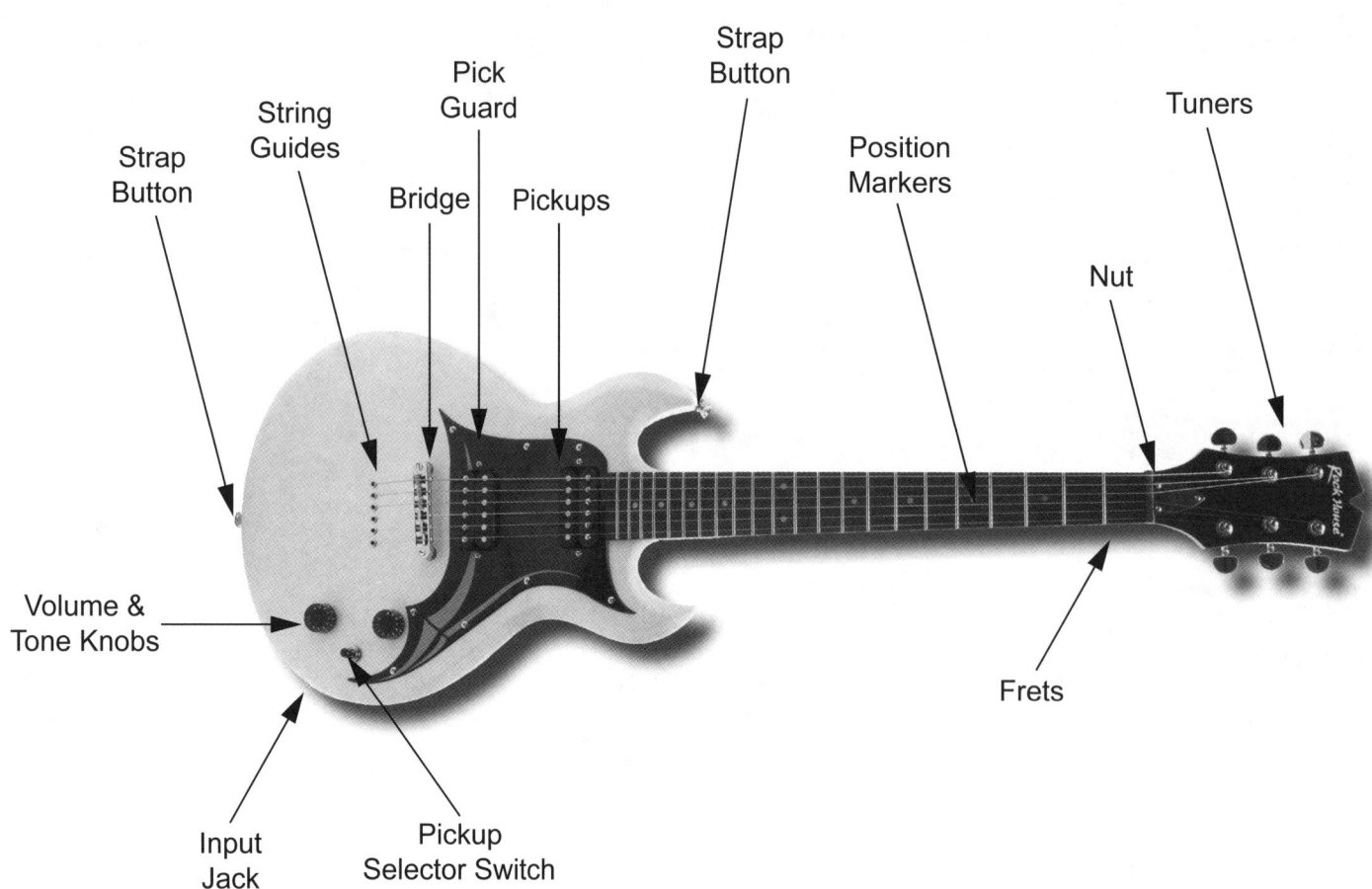

Holding the Guitar

Throughout this book, we will refer to the picking hand as your right hand, and the hand fretting the notes as your left hand. If you are left handed and playing a left handed guitar, just make the necessary adjustments as you follow along (read "right hand" to mean your left hand and vice versa).

The photos below show the proper way to hold a guitar. Rest the body of the guitar on your right leg when sitting. When standing, attach a guitar strap to the strap buttons and wear the strap over your left shoulder. Locate the input jack on your guitar. Before you plug in, turn the volume down on the guitar; the amplifier should be off. Plug the cord into the guitar and the amplifier, then turn the amp on and bring up the volume.

Rest the guitar on your right leg when seated.

When standing, the guitar strap goes over your left shoulder.

Be sure the amplifier is turned off before you plug in.

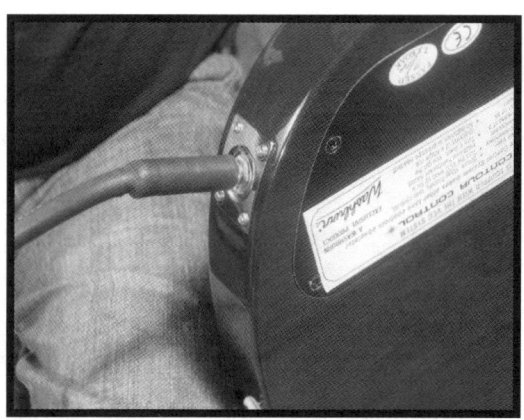

Insert the cord all the way into the input jack.

Holding the Pick

Hold the pick between the index finger and thumb of your right hand. Leave just the tip pointing out, perpendicular to your thumb. Your thumb and finger should be placed in the center of the pick, grasping it firmly to give you good control. Leave your hand open (don't make a fist) and let the rest of your fingers hang loosely.

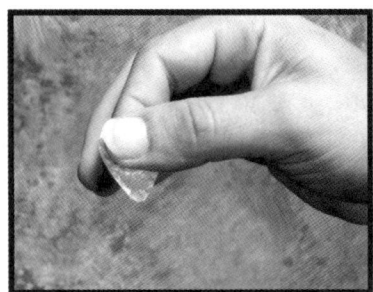

Grasp the pick between your index finger and thumb.

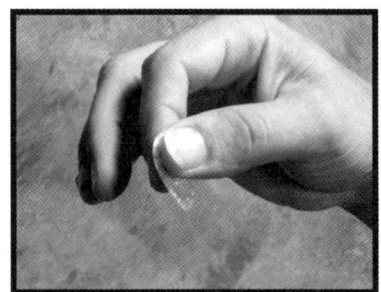

Leave your hand open and your other fingers loose.

To properly position the pick, center the pick on your index finger (Fig. 1) and bring your thumb down on top of it (Fig. 2). Pinch your thumb and finger together and leave just the tip of the pick showing (Fig. 3).

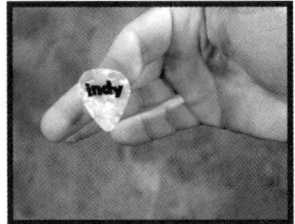

Fig. 1

Fig. 2

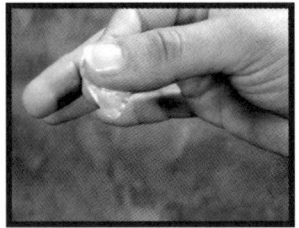

Fig. 3

Right Hand Position

Place your right arm on the very top of the guitar and let it drape down almost parallel to the bridge (Fig. 4). Leave part of your hand or fingers touching the guitar's body and keep them anchored to the guitar (Fig. 5). This will help give your picking hand a reference point.

Fig. 4

Fig. 5

Left Hand Position

Hold your left hand out in front of you with your wrist straight (Fig. 6). Curl your fingers in and just naturally bring your hand back to the neck of the guitar (Figs. 7 & 8). Try not to bend or contort your wrist. Your fingers should stay curled inward; most of the time only your fingertips will touch the strings when playing. The first joint of your thumb should be in the middle of the back of the neck (Fig. 9). Try to avoid touching the neck with any other part of your hand. Make sure you have the proper right and left hand positions down so that when we progress you'll have no problems.

Fig. 6

Fig. 7

Fig. 8

Fig. 9

Essential Blues Tools

Solid Body Electric Guitar

The solid body electric is the standard electric guitar that's great for distortion sounds and lead playing. Pickups mounted on the guitar's body send the sound to an amplifier. If there are two (or more) pickups, a pickup selector switch (toggle switch) is used to select one or blend them together. Pickups located near the bridge (bridge pickups) tend to have a brighter sound, making them better suited for lead playing. Pickups closer to the neck (neck pickups) have a warmer sound, making them a good choice for rhythm playing. A humbucker pickup is a popular double coil pickup designed to cancel electronic hum.

Acoustic Guitar

An acoustic guitar is an ideal choice for intimate performances, classic blues, fingerpicking, country, or bluegrass. The sound is projected out from the body of the guitar through the sound hole, making an amplifier unnecessary. An acoustic/electric is a type of acoustic guitar with built in pickups, allowing it to be amplified through an amp or PA system.

Hollow Body Electric Guitar

A hollow body electric guitar is a hybrid of the regular acoustic and electric guitars. It has F-holes on the front of the body, allowing the sound to resonate. These guitars are the choice of many classic blues and slide guitarists.

Picks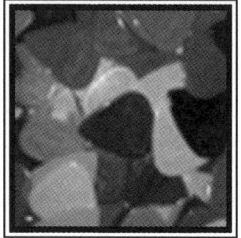

There are many different types of picks in different thicknesses. A heavy pick may offer you more control for lead playing, but medium and light picks have a flexibility that's good for rhythm playing. I suggest that you have a selection of different pick thicknesses available and experiment with them in lead and rhythm applications.

Strings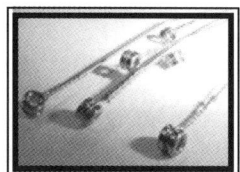

Strings are available in different gauges. Heavier gauge strings produce a thicker, fuller sound; lighter gauges are thinner, easier to bend and great for soloing.

Tuning

Each of the six strings on a guitar is tuned to and named after a different note (pitch). The thinnest or 1st string is referred to as the highest string because it is the highest sounding string. The thickest or 6th string is referred to as the lowest string because it is the lowest sounding string. Memorize the names of the open strings. These notes form the basis for finding any other notes on the guitar.

Names of the Open Strings

6th string	5th string	4th string	3rd string	2nd string	1st string
E	A	D	G	B	E

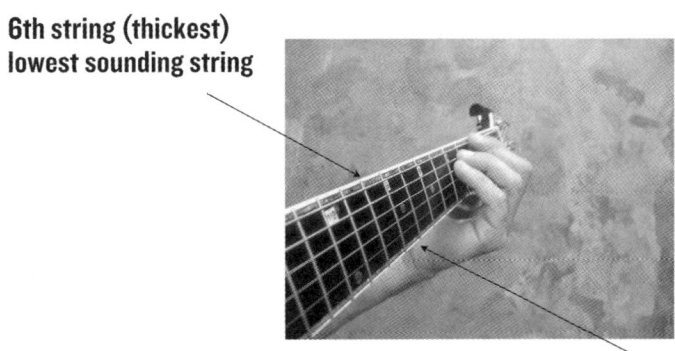

6th string (thickest) lowest sounding string

1st string (thinnest) highest sounding string

Tune your guitar using the machine heads on the headstock. Turn the machine heads a little bit at a time while plucking the string and listening to the change in pitch. Tighten the string to raise the pitch. Loosen the string to lower the pitch. Be careful not to accidentally break a string by tightening it too much or too quickly.

The easiest way to tune a guitar is to use an electronic tuner. There are many different kinds available that are fairly inexpensive. You can also download the free online tuner from RockHouseMethod.com.

Reading Chord Charts

A chord is a group of notes played together. A chord chart (chord diagram) is a graphic representation of part of the fretboard (as if you stood the guitar up from floor to ceiling and looked directly at the front of the neck). The vertical lines represent the strings; the horizontal lines represent the frets.

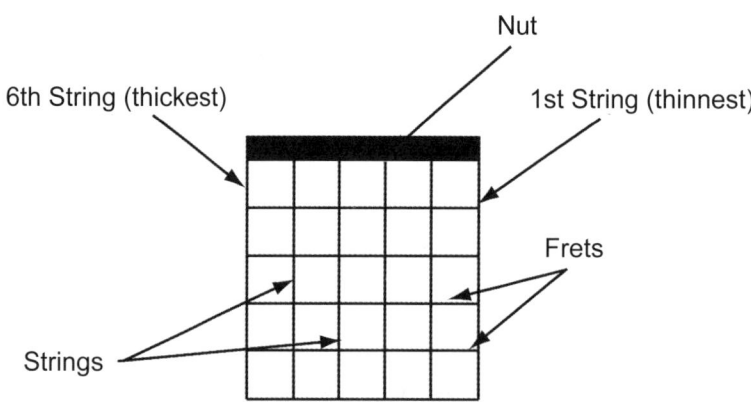

Chord diagrams show which notes to play and which strings they are played on. The black dots within the graph represent fretted notes and show you where your fingers should go. Each of these dots will have a number inside of it. These numbers indicate which left hand finger to fret the note with (1 = index, 2 = middle, 3 = ring, 4 = pinky). The 0s at the top of the diagram show which strings are played open (strummed with no left hand fingers touching them). The Xs at the top of the diagram show which strings are not played.

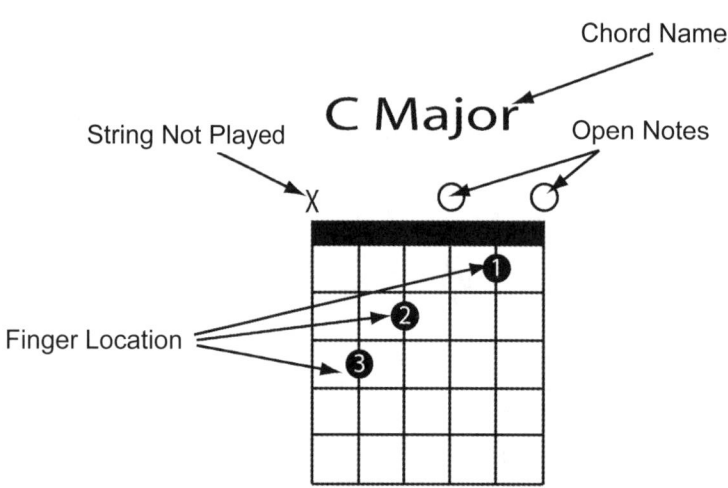

For each dot (or fretted note,) follow this sequence; finger - fret - string. In the diagram above the dot furthest to the right would be the 1st finger, on the first fret, on the second string. Use this pattern sequence for each dot to fret the entire chord.

Open Blues Chords

Open Major Chords

The following open major chords are the most commonly used in rock and blues progressions. These three chords, A, D, and E, represent the I - IV - V (one - four - five) chords in the key of A major. The roman numerals refer to the steps of the scale, relative to what key the music is in. The A chord is the I chord (also called the tonic). The D chord is the IV chord (also called the subdominant) because in the key of A, D is the fourth step of the scale. Finally, the V chord (or dominant) is the E chord, because E is the fifth step of the scale in the key of A. To find the I - IV - V chords in any key, build chords on the 1st, 4th and 5th degrees of the scale.

The I - IV - V chord progression is the foundation that all rock and blues was built on and has evolved from. There are many variations, but songs such as "Johnny B. Goode," "You Really Got Me," "Rock and Roll," "I Love Rock and Roll" and "Sympathy for the Devil" are all based on the I - IV - V.

In the A chord diagram, the slur going across the notes means you should barre (bar) those notes. A barre is executed by placing one finger flat across more than one string. Pick each note of the chord individually to make sure you're applying enough pressure with your finger. Notice that the 6th and 1st strings each have an "x" below them on the diagram, indicating these strings are not played (either muted or not strummed). For each chord, the first photo shows what the chord looks like from the front. The second photo is from the player's perspective.

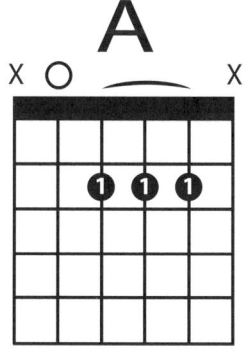

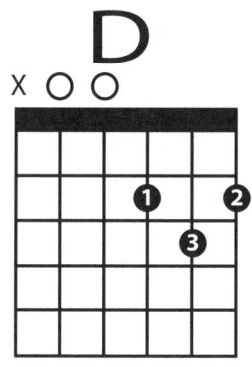

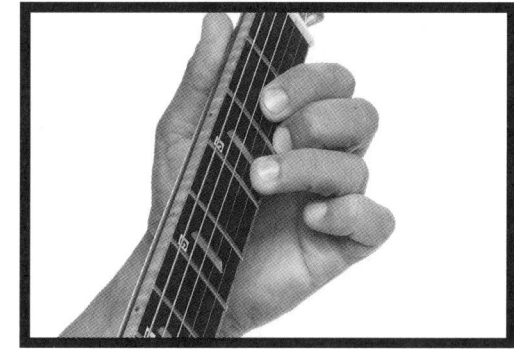

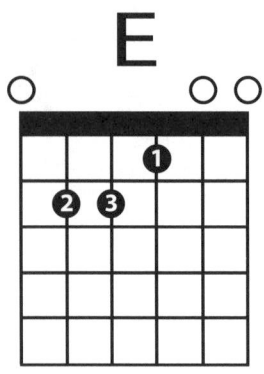

Open Minor Chords

Here are the I - IV - V chords in the key of A minor: Am, Dm and Em. Minor chords have a sad or melancholy sound, whereas the major chords have a bright or happy sound

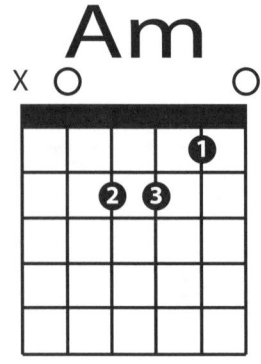
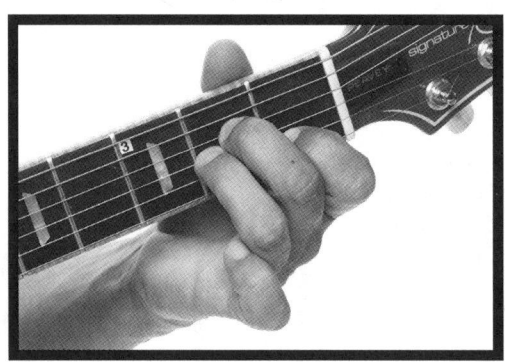

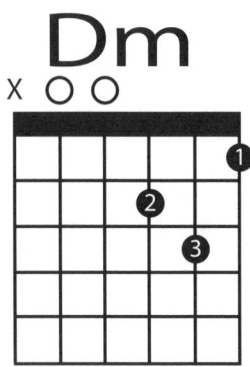

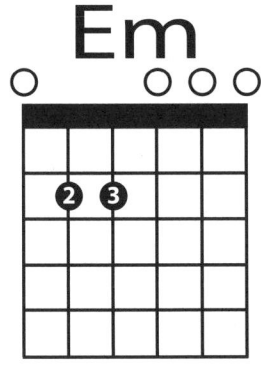

Be sure to use proper left hand technique when playing chords for maximum tone and control. Remember to keep your thumb firmly anchored against the back of the neck. Your fingers should be curled inward toward the fretboard and only the tips of your fingers should be touching the strings. Don't grab the neck with your whole hand; no other parts of your fingers or hand should be touching the neck or any of the other strings. Place your fingertips just to the left of (behind) the fret, pressing the strings inward toward the neck. When strumming chords, pivot from your elbow and keep your wrist straight; the strumming motion should come from your elbow and wrist. When playing single notes, use more wrist.

One of the hardest things for a beginner to conquer is the ability to play a clean, fully sustained chord without buzzing strings, muted or dead notes. Make sure your left hand is fretting the proper notes and your fingers aren't accidentally touching any of the other strings. Pick each string individually with your right hand, one note at a time. If any of the open strings are deadened or muted, try slightly adjusting your fingers. If any of the fretted notes are buzzing, you probably aren't pressing down hard enough with your fingers. It will be difficult at first and might hurt a little, but don't get discouraged. With time and practice, you'll build up callouses on your fingertips. Before you know it, playing chords will be second nature and your fingers will hardly feel it at all.

Once you have the chords sounding clean and the strumming motion down, the next step is to learn how to change chords quickly and cleanly. Focus on where each finger needs to move for the next chord. Sometimes one or more of your fingers will be able to stay in the same place. Avoid taking your hand completely off the neck. Instead, try to move your whole hand as little as possible and make smaller finger adjustments to change from one chord to the next. When you can change from chord to chord seamlessly, you'll be able to play complete songs.

Quick Quote!

> "Between sets I'd sneak over to the black places to hear blues musicians. It got to the point where I was making my living at white clubs and having my fun at the other places."
>
> - Stevie Ray Vaughan

Open Chord Blues

The following is an example of a chord progression and is written on a musical staff. A staff is the group of horizontal lines on which music is written. The chord names written above the staff show which chord to play in this case A minor and E minor, and the rhythm slashes indicate the rhythm in which the chords are strummed. A chord progression is a series of chords played in a specified rhythm and order. In this progression, strum each chord eight times, using all downstrums. This example also uses repeat signs (play through the progression and repeat it again). Always count along out loud with each strum, in time and on the beat. Start out slowly if you need to and gradually get it up to speed.

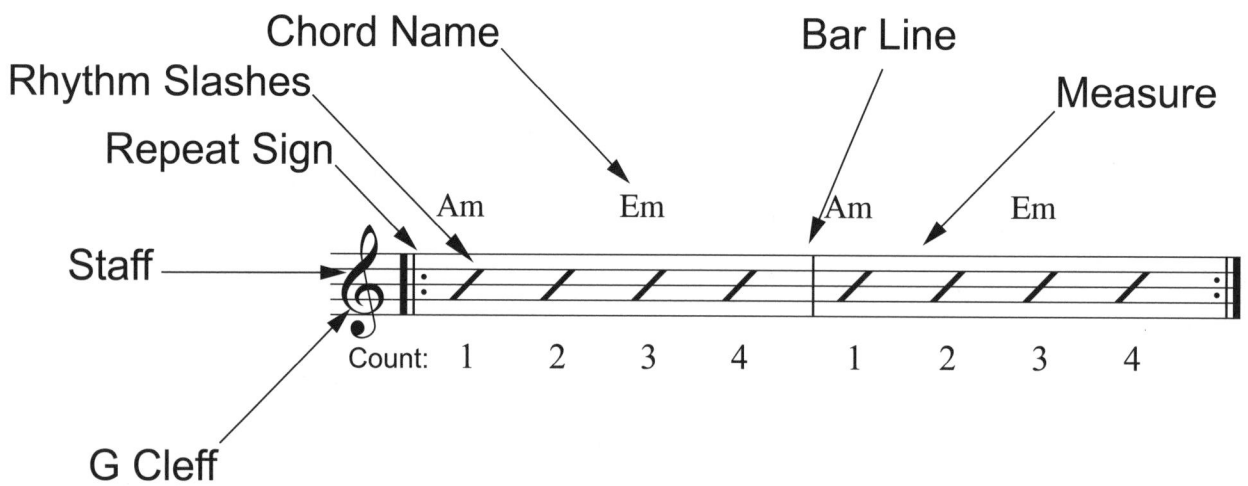

Definition of Terms

Staff: The most frequently used staff has five horizontal lines, with four spaces, upon which the notes and other musical symbols are placed.

Measure: The space between two bar lines on a staff.

Rest: A symbol used to designate silence.

Clef: A symbol placed at the beginning of the staff to indicate the pitch of the notes on the staff. The G clef is the clef used for all guitar music

Chord: A combination of three or more tones sounded simultaneously.

Repeat Sign: A sign used to designate repeating a section of music. There will be one at the begining and one at the end of the section to be repeated..

Rhythm: These slashes represent strums and tell how you should play the chords. .

Here are the two open chord Blues progressions. Listen and play along with the backing track to hear how they should should sound. Keep practicing and try to change chords in time without stalling or missing a beat. Count along out loud with each strum, in time and on the beat. Start out slowly if you need to and gradually get it up to speed using a metronome.

A Major

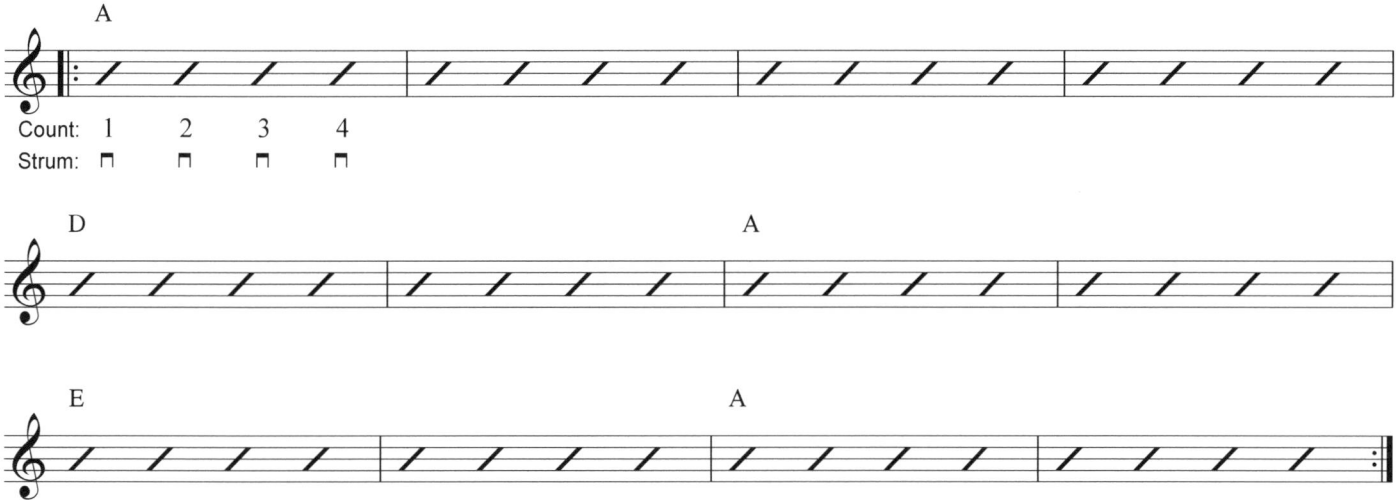

A Minor

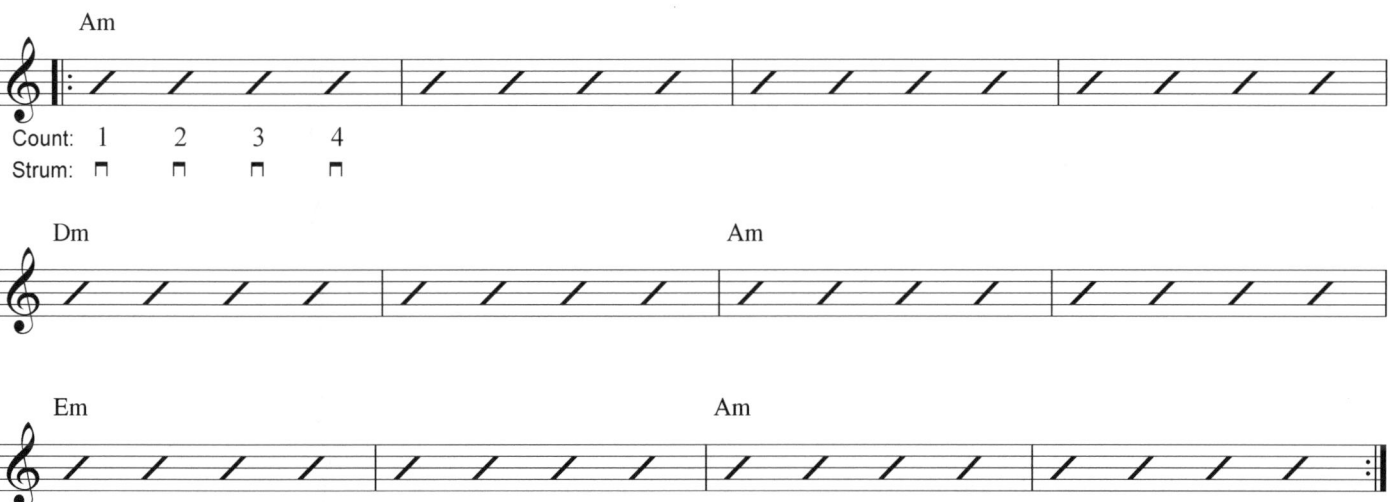

When playing through these two progressions, listen to the tonal quality of each. The Major progression has a happy sound and the minor progression has a sad or melancholy tonality. This is due to the tonal quality of the chord types. Minor chords are sad sounding and Major chords have a bright, happy or powerful sound to them.

Reading Tab

Tablature (or tab) is a number system for reading notes on the guitar. The six lines of the tablature staff represent each of the strings on the guitar. The top line is the thinnest (highest pitched) string. The numbers placed directly on these lines are the fret number to play each note. Underneath the staff, is a series of numbers that tell you which left hand finger to fret the notes with. The tablature staff is divided into a small sections called measures by bar lines.

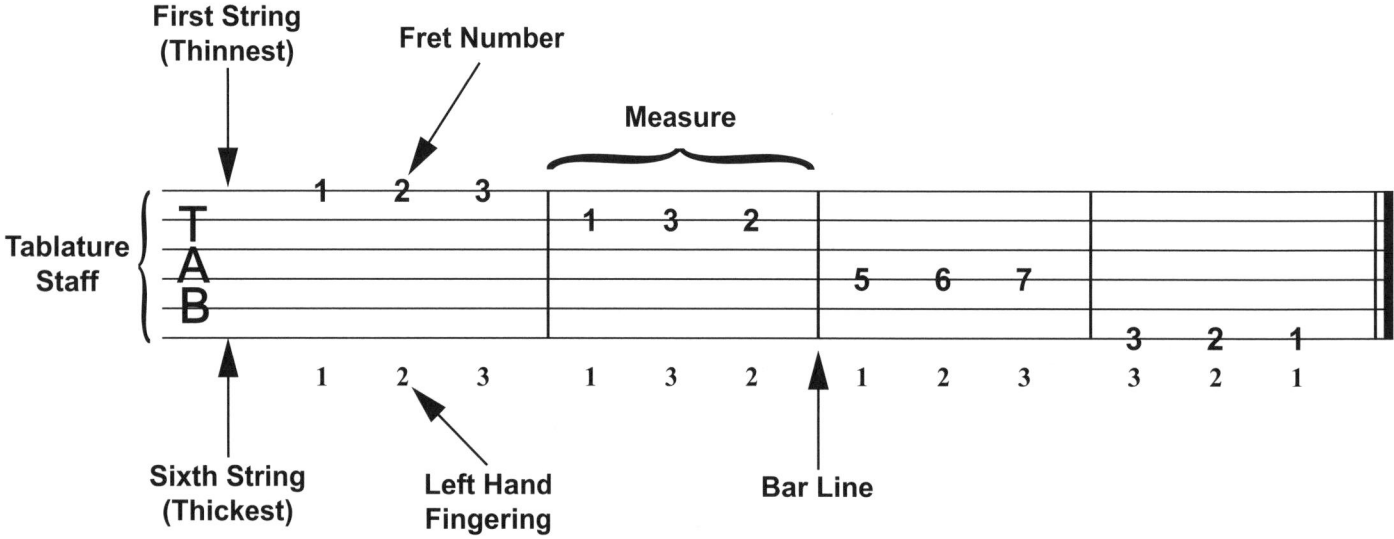

Chords can also be written in tab. If there are several numbers stacked together in a column, those notes should be played or strummed at the same time. Here are the Am and Em chords with the tablature written out underneath each diagram. Since the fingerings are shown on the chord diagrams, we won't bother to repeat them underneath the tab.

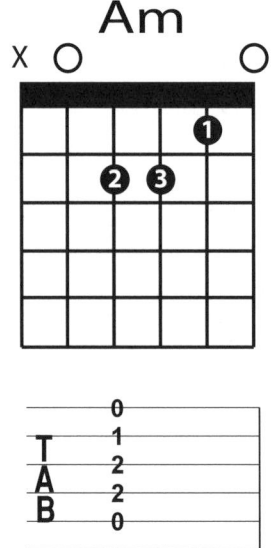
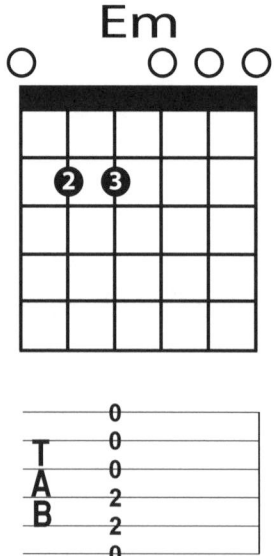

Basic Blues Rhythm

The following is a basic blues rhythm in the key of A. This rhythm is made up of two note chords shown on the tab staff. The chord names above the staff are there as a reference to show you what the full chord that corresponds is while you play along.

This rihythm should sound very familiar - it's used more than any other blues progression. Plenty of rock and blues classics are played entirely with this one rhythm repeated over and over. It is made up of 12 measures (or bars) of music, called the 12-bar blues, a blues progression consisting of twelve repeated bars of music.

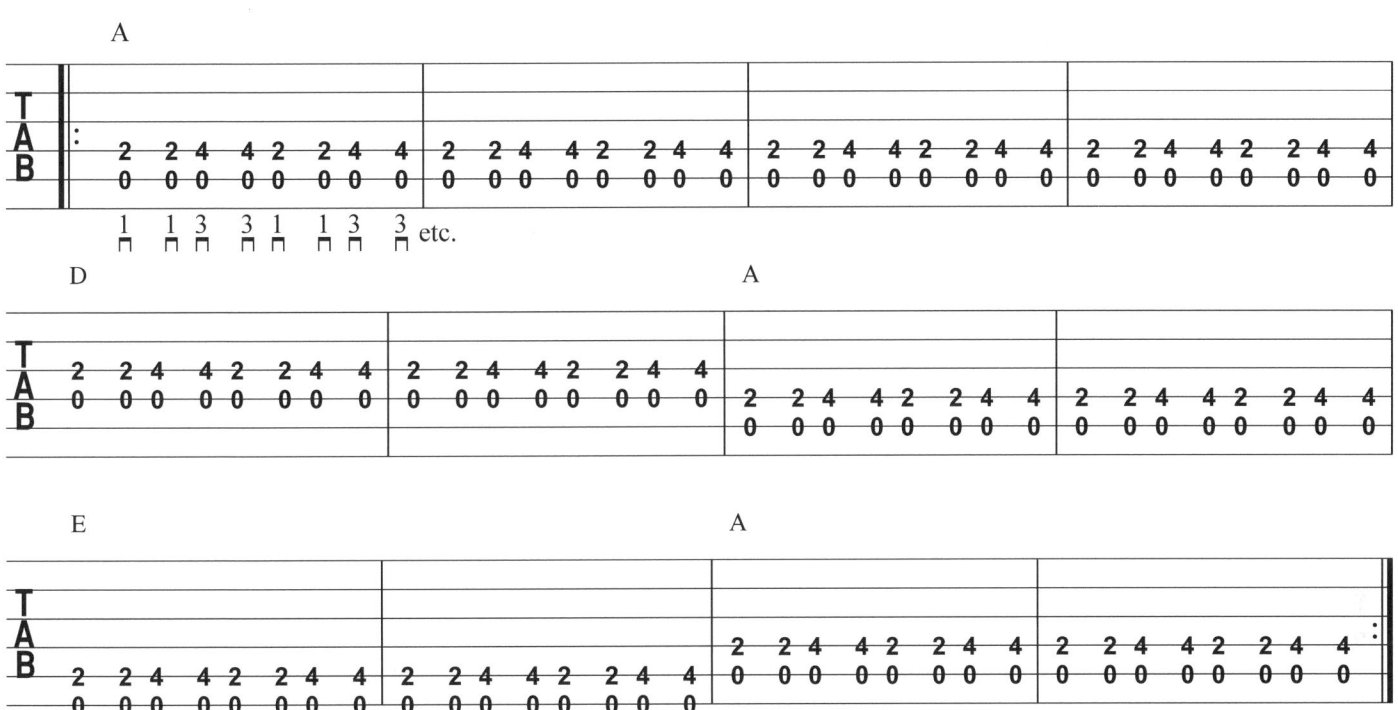

Counting Beats

A beat is the basic unit of time in music. A common way to count beats is to tap your foot. One beat would equal tapping your foot down-up. Tap your foot and count 1 – 2 – 3 – 4 repetitively, say each number as your foot hits the ground. You will learn different note types that tell you how many beats to let notes ring.

Foot Down

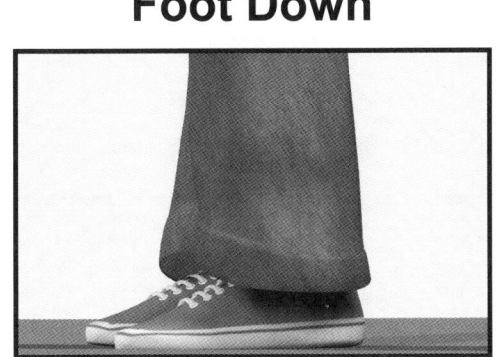

Foot Up

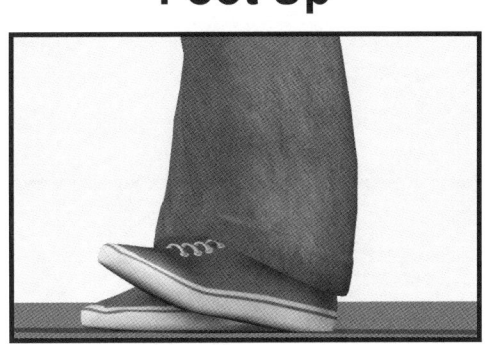

The Blues Shuffle

Blues is played with a shuffle feel, also called a triplet feel. The previous example can be played with a straight feel or a shuffle feel. For the shuffle feel the second eighth note of each beat should lag a little. This is referred to as triplet feel because the beat is actually divided by thirds, counted as if there were three eighth notes per beat instead of two. The first part of the beat gets 2/3 of a beat, and the second part only gets 1/3.

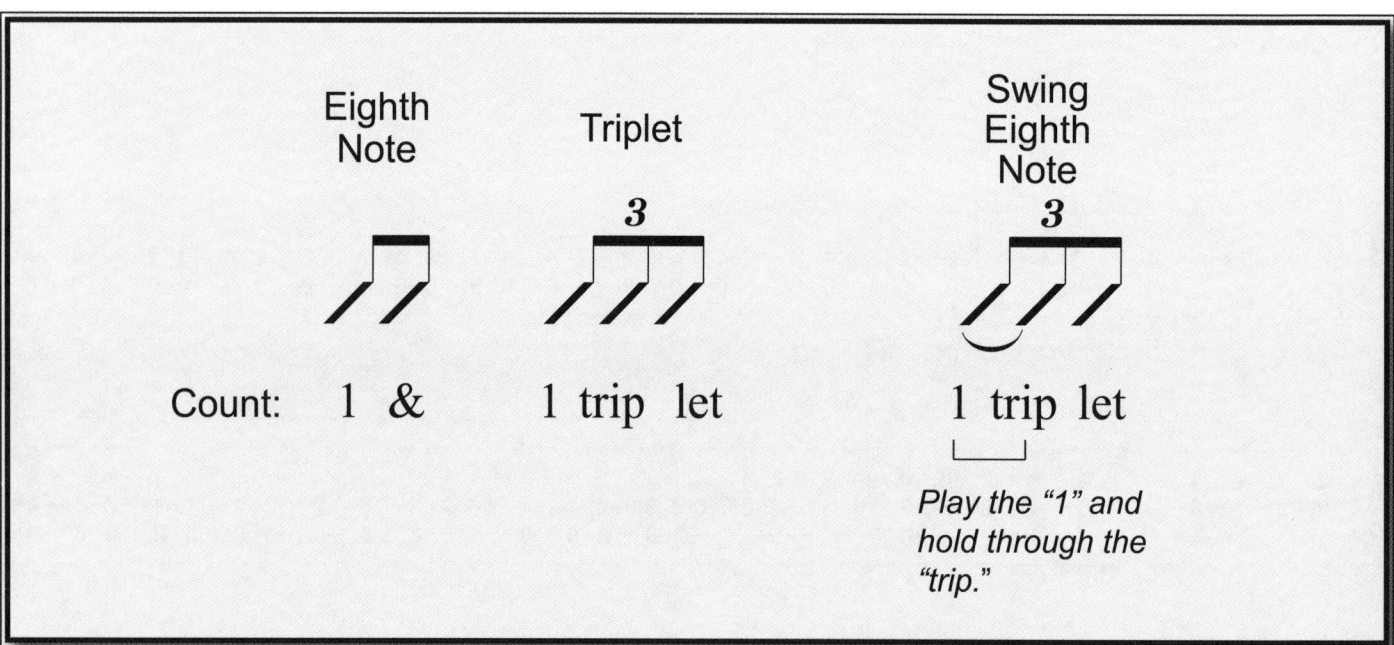

Shuffle feel is a much easier concept to understand by hearing it. Listen to the backing track, count along and try to get the triplet feel in your head. Also, check out almost any blues standard, slow or fast, and you'll probably recognize a shuffle feel being used.

Quick Quote!

"Blues is easy to play, but hard to feel."

- Jimi Hendrix

Reading a Scale Diagram

Scale diagrams are simply a diagram outlining where the notes of a scale are located on the guitar neck. The six lines that go from left to right represent each of the six strings. Like with tablature, the top line is the thinnest (highest pitched) string and the bottom line is the thickest (lowest pitched) string. The lines running from top to bottom are the frets. The numbered dots placed directly on a string show you the specific fret to play each note, and the number inside indicates which left hand finger to fret the note with. The numbers underneath the diagram indicate where on the neck the scale is located, in this diagram the scale begins at the 5th fret:

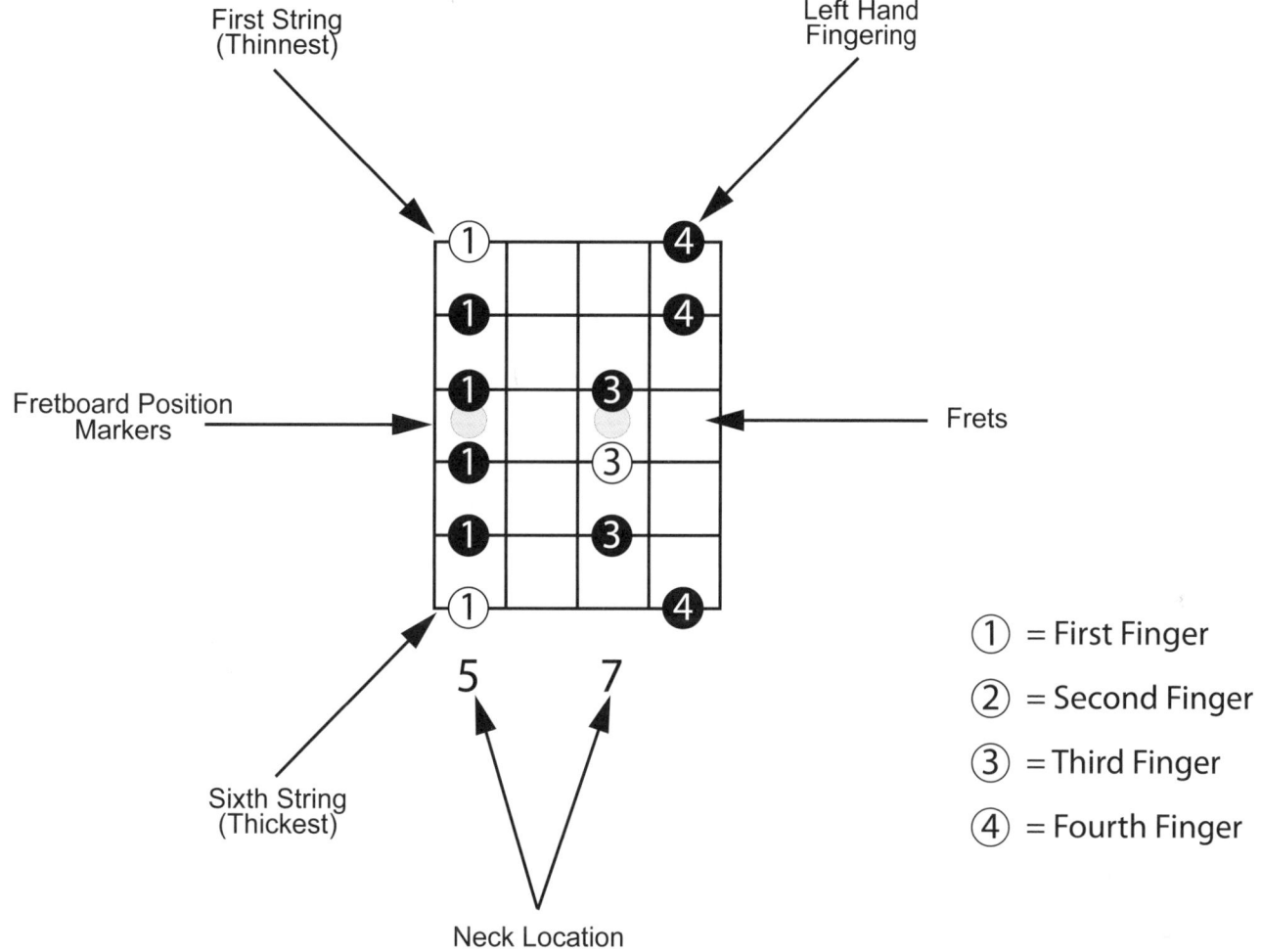

Notice how the diagram above is a mirror image of the guitar neck. Below see how this scale pattern looks on the guitar.

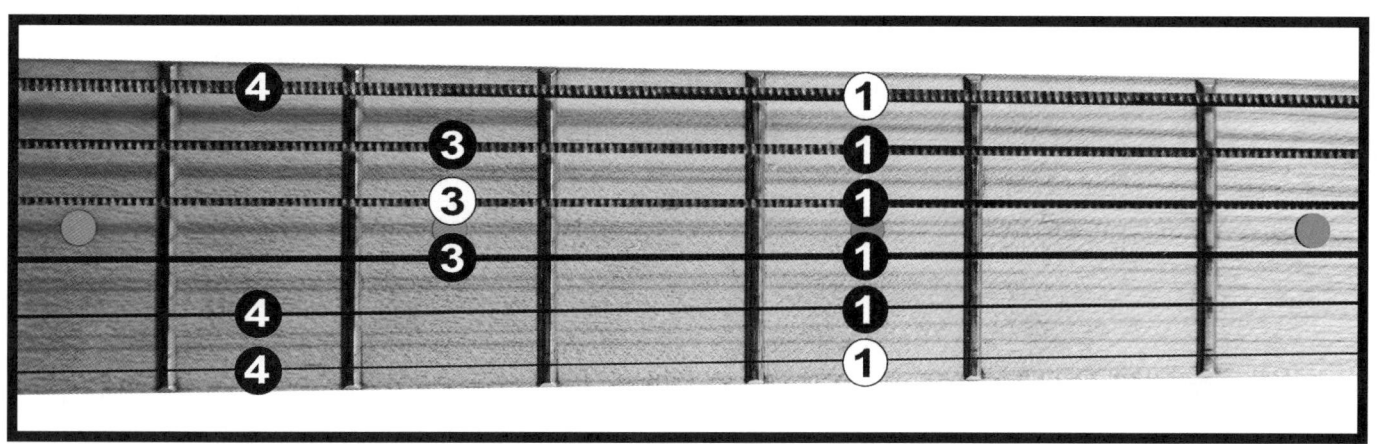

23

Minor Pentatonic Scales
Key of "A"

Minor pentatonic scales are the most commonly used scales for playing rock and blues solos. The pentatonic is a five note scale, or an abbreviated version of the full natural minor scale that you will learn later in this program. The word "pentatonic" comes from the greek words, "penta" (five) and "tonic" (the keynote). The five notes found in the minor pentatonic scale in the key of "A" are A - C - D - E - G.

Memorize and practice this scale; it's the one you'll use most often for playing melodies and leads. There are five different positions of this scale, each beginning on a different note of the scale. All five positions are shown here in tab. To the right of each tab staff is a scale diagram. These are similar to the chord diagrams we've previously used. A scale diagram shows you all the notes in the scale within a certain position on the neck.

☐ = Root Note

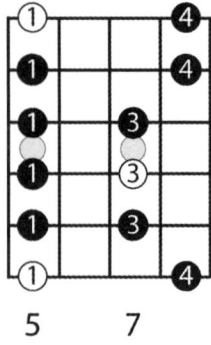

1st Position

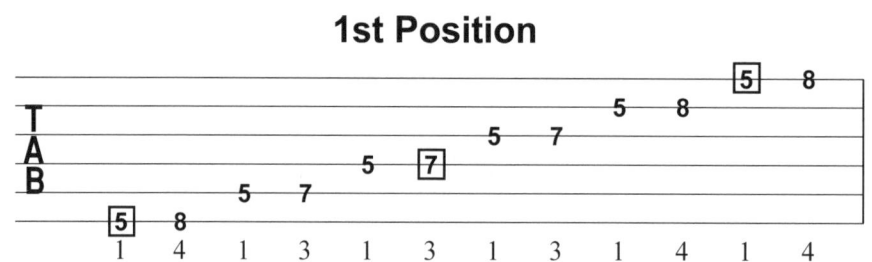

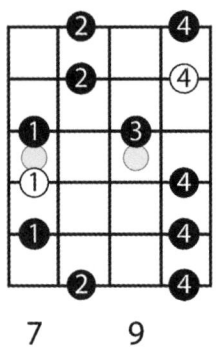

2nd Position

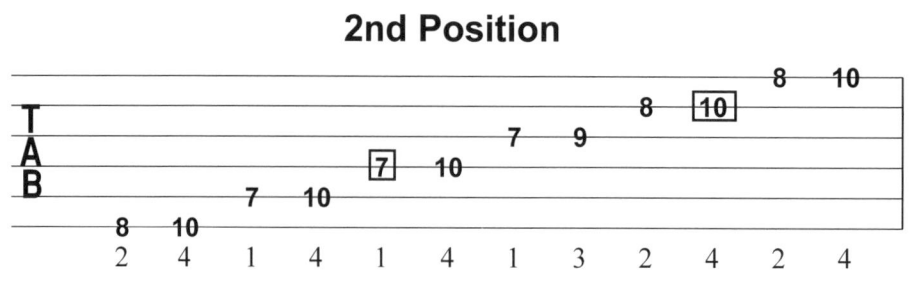

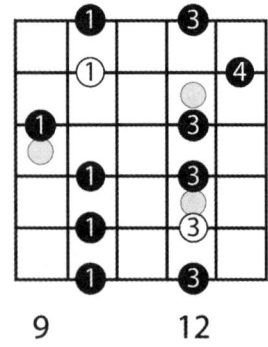

3rd Position

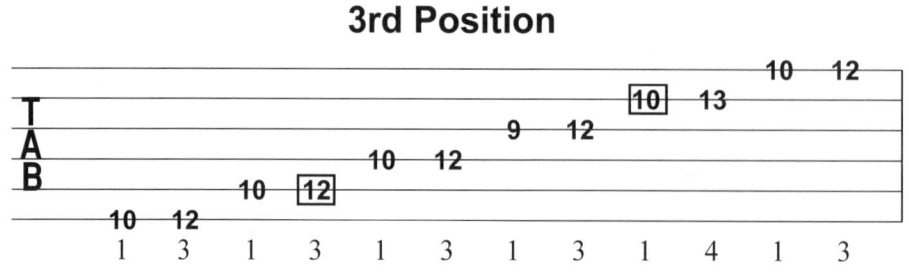

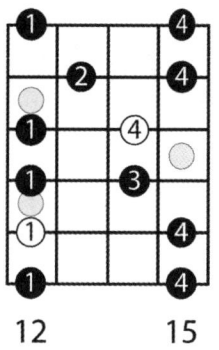

4th Position

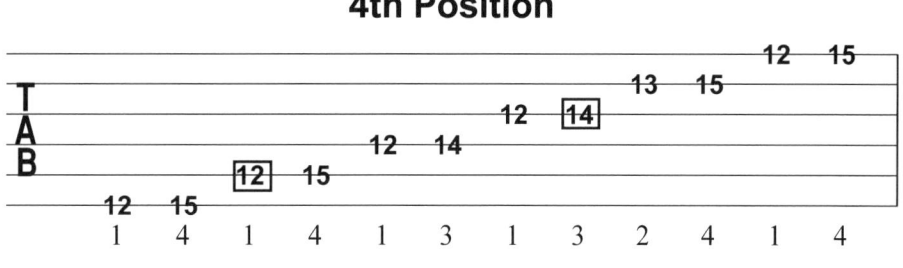

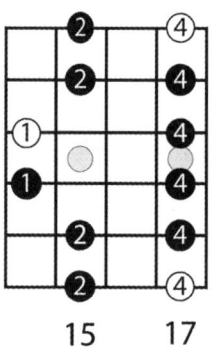

5th Position

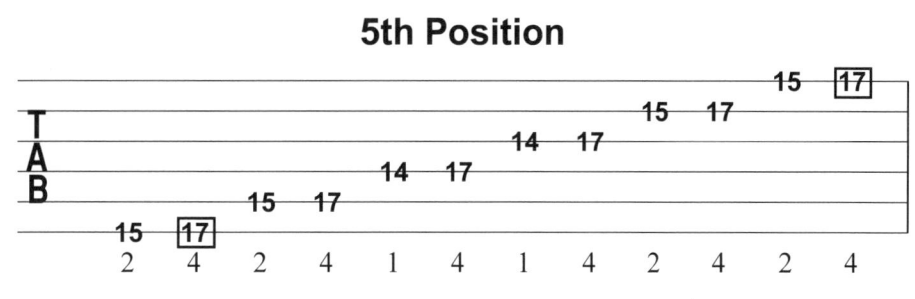

"A" Minor Pentatonic Fretboard Diagram

Once you have all five positions of the minor pentatonic scales mastered, you'll be able to play solos in any position on the neck. Remember that there are only five different name notes in the scale A - C - D - E - G, and the different positions are just groupings of these same notes in different octaves and different places on the neck. The 4th and 5th positions from the previous page can be transposed one octave lower (shown below in the fretboard diagram). Notice how each position overlaps the next; the left side of one position is the right side of the next one and so on. Think of these scale positions as building blocks (like Legos). When soloing, you can move from position to position and play across the entire fretboard.

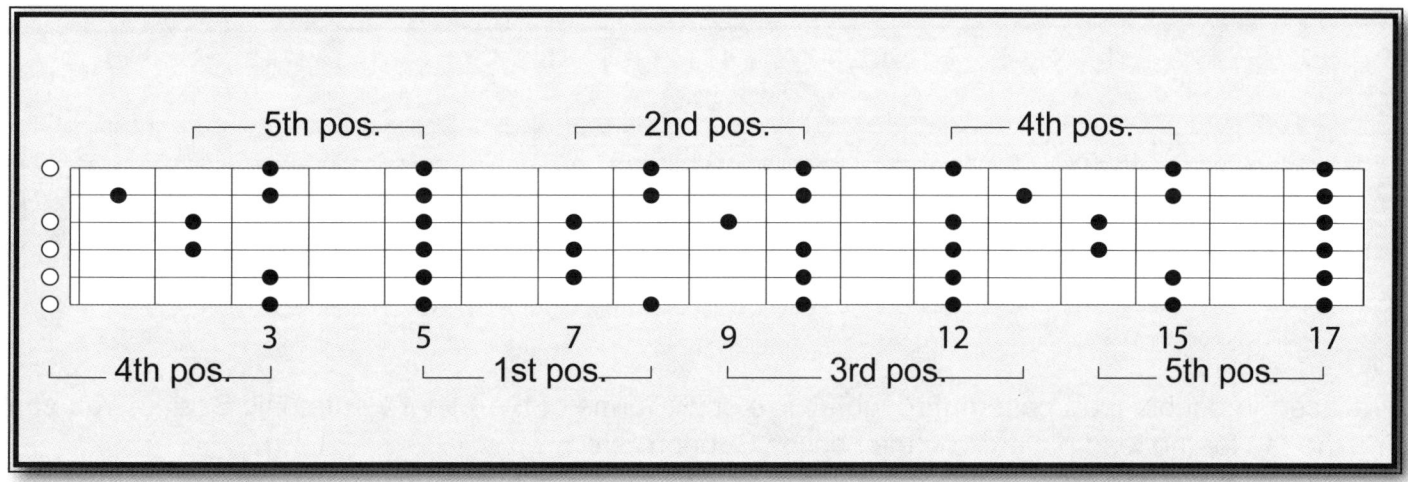

Lead Patterns

The following examples are standard lead pattern exercises, designed to help you build coordination and learn how to use the minor pentatonic scales for playing leads. Use alternate picking and the metronome and start out slowly to get the rhythm. Memorize the patterns and gradually speed up the tempo. Before you know it, you'll be playing blazing rock and blues guitar solos.

The Double Lead Pattern

1st Position

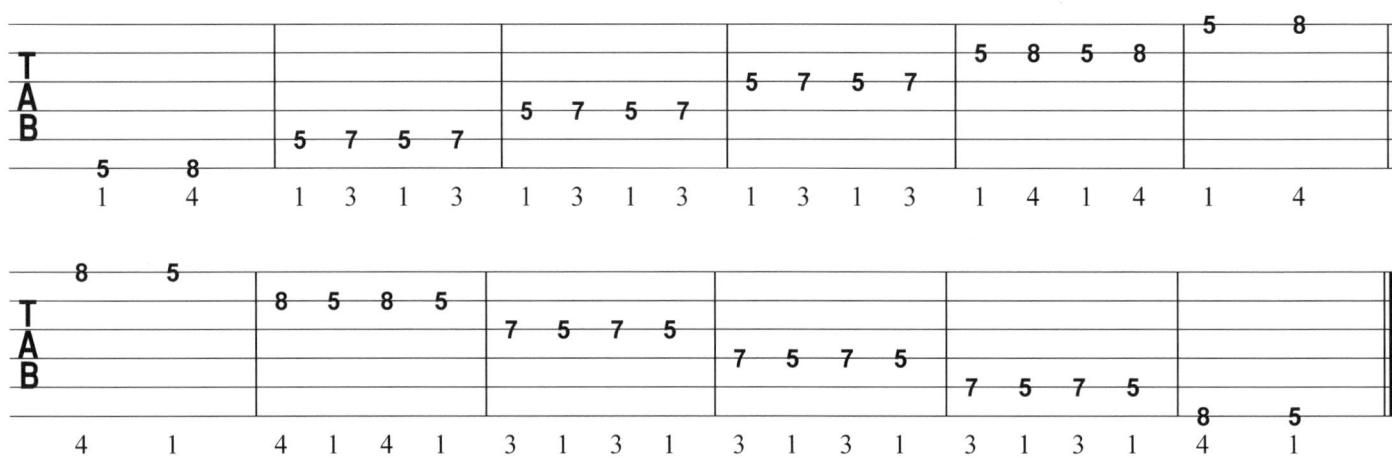

2nd Position

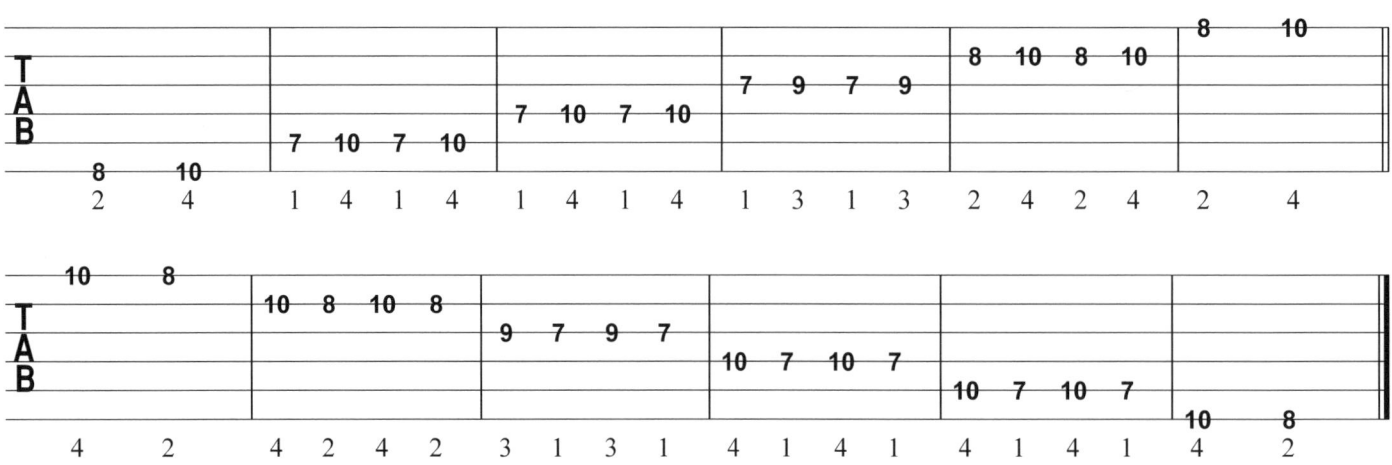

Practice the double lead pattern through all five scale forms of the Minor Pentatonic Scales. You can find the tab for the lead patterns on the Lesson Support Site.

The Triplet Lead Pattern

1st Position

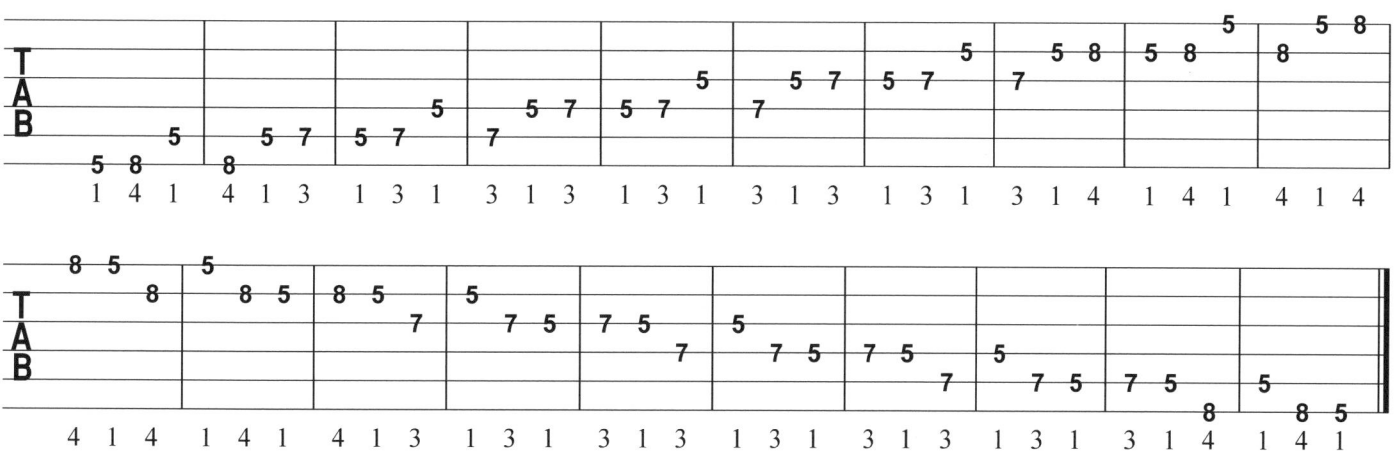

2nd Position

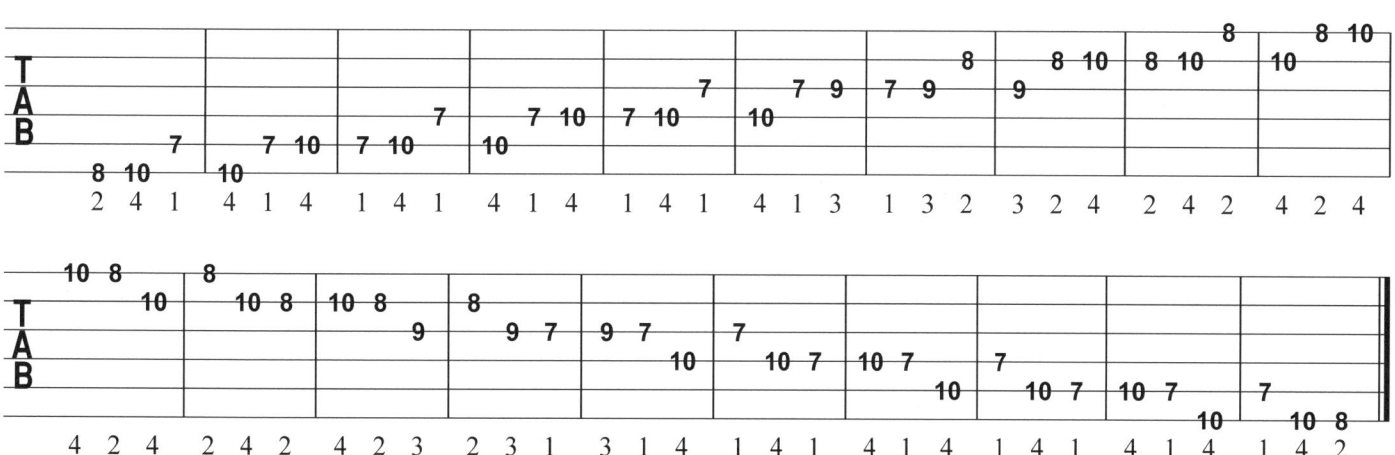

Practice the triplet lead pattern through all five scale forms of the Minor Pentatonic Scales. You can find the tab for the lead patterns on the Lesson Support Site.

Quick Quote!

"Blues is a natural fact, is something that a fellow lives. If you don't live it you don't have it. Young people have forgotten to cry the blues. Now they talk and get lawyers and things."

- Big Bill Broonzy

Bends

Now let's learn some lead guitar techniques that will add expression to your playing. Bends are a very soulful way of creating emotion with the guitar, using flesh against steel to alter and control pitches. All guitarists have their own unique, signature way of bending notes.

The row of tab staffs below show bends using the third, fourth or first fingers. The arrow above the note indicates a bend, and the arrow with the word "full" above it means to bend the note one whole step in pitch.

First try the third finger bend. While fretting the note with your third finger, keep your first two fingers down on the string behind it and push upward using all three fingers. This will give you added coordination and control. Use the same technique for the fourth finger bend, using all four fingers to bend the string upward. The first finger bend will probably be the hardest since you are only using one finger to bend the string. In some situations, you may even pull the string downward with your first finger to bend the note.

Third Finger Bend

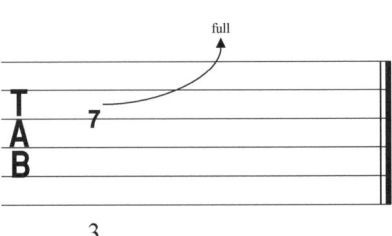

3

Fourth Finger Bend

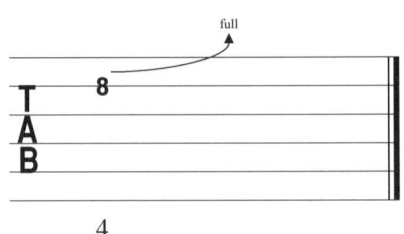

4

First Finger Bend

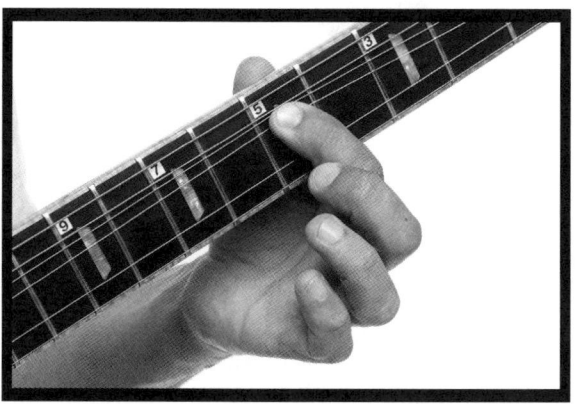
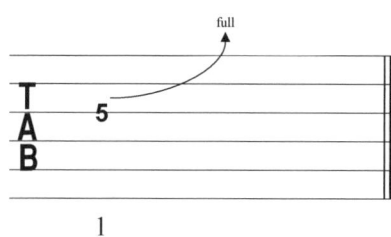

The following exercises show what bending looks like in context when playing a solo using the 1st position A minor pentatonic scale. Play through these exercises and start to get a feel for how to incorporate bends into your own riffs.

Example 1

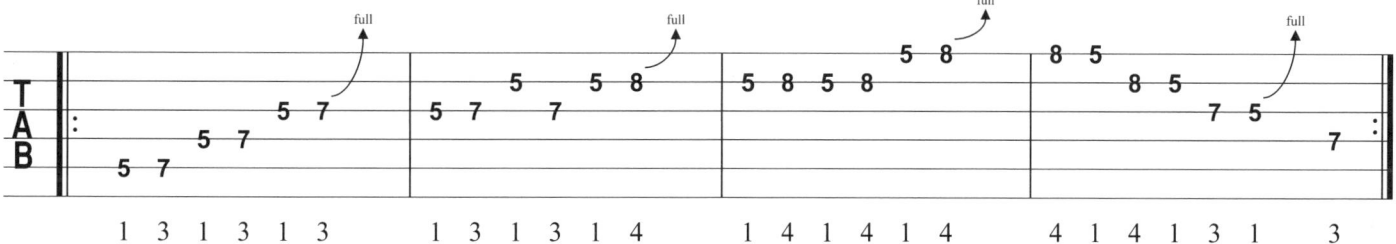

Example 2

The following example incorporates a half step bend. Bend the first note up only one half step or one fret this is indicated by the arrow and "1/2" above the note. Half step bends are commonly used in blues leads so get familiar with them.

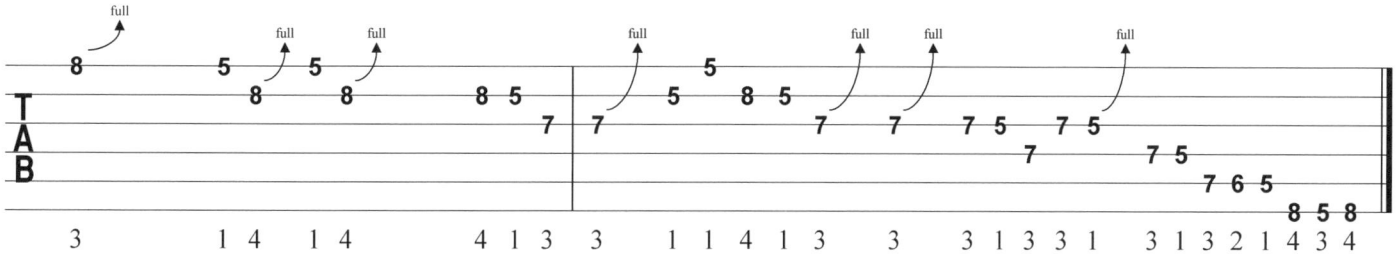

29

Hammer ons

Hammer ons are a widely used lead guitar technique. On the staff below, you'll see curved lines or slurs connecting tab notes. This indicates that you'll be picking the first note, but not picking the second note. The second note will be sounded by pushing your finger down in a hammer like fashion to make the sound resonate.

So the first tab note is picked, and the second note is not. The H on top of that note represents the hammer-on note. The first hammer-on exercise uses your first and third finger on the 4th and 3rd strings, and your 1st and 4th finger on the 2nd string. Remember pick the first note, which is your 1st finger and hammer it on the second note, which is either your 3rd or 4th finger. Read the tablature, take your time, and really get used to the hammer-on technique because it is widely used for lead guitar.

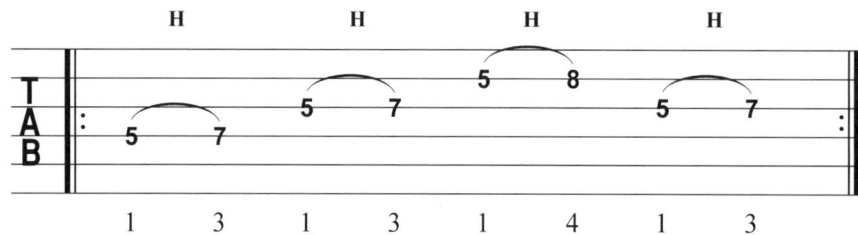

The second exercise uses the minor pentatonic scale 1st position in a pattern. This pattern goes down in three string intervals starting with the 6th, 5th and 4th strings, then 5th, 4th, 3rd strings, 4th, 3rd, 2nd strings, and then 3rd, 2nd, and 1st strings.

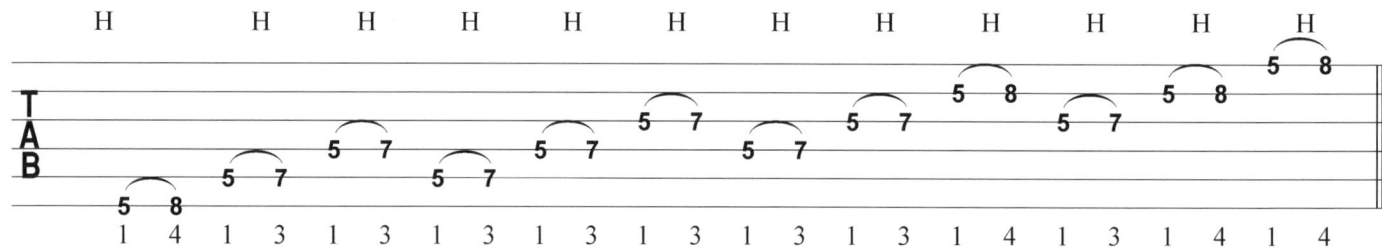

Pull offs

Pull offs are the opposite of hammer ons. Pick the first note and pull or snap your finger off the string to the get the second note. Your first finger should already be in place, fretting the second note in advance. The "P" above each slur below indicates a pull off.

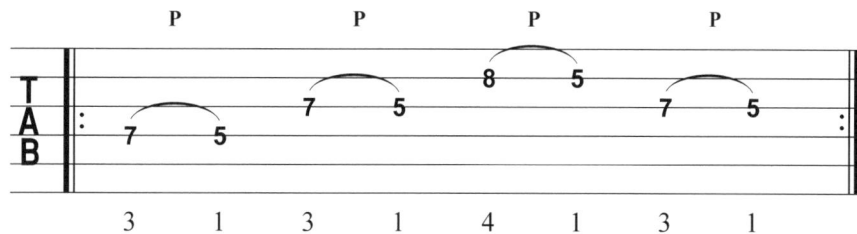

The second example pulls off through the 1st position minor pentatonic scale. It starts at the first string and goes down in three string intervals. After you can play the pull offs with the 1st position scale play this pattern with the other four positions.

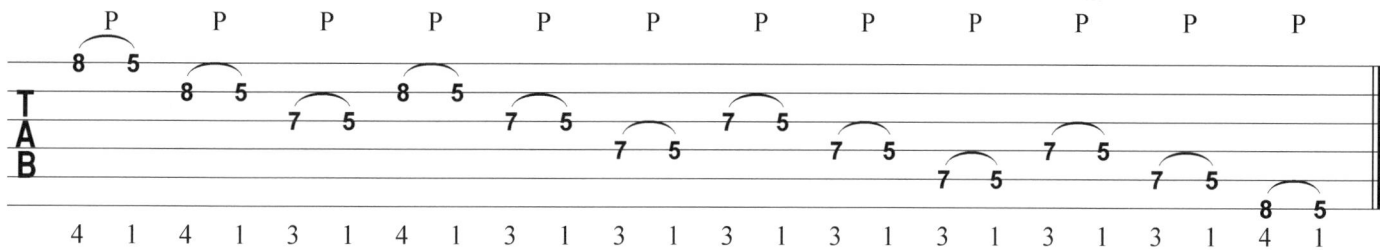

Full Blues Lead

Here's an example of a solo that can be played over the shuffle blues rhythm you've learned previously. This solo incorporates bends, hammer ons and pull offs in a variety of positions. The riff in the first measure is one of the most commonly used blues riffs; it can be heard in countless blues guitar solos. After you've got this solo down, try to create your own using the different lead techniques and all five positions of the A minor pentatonic scales.

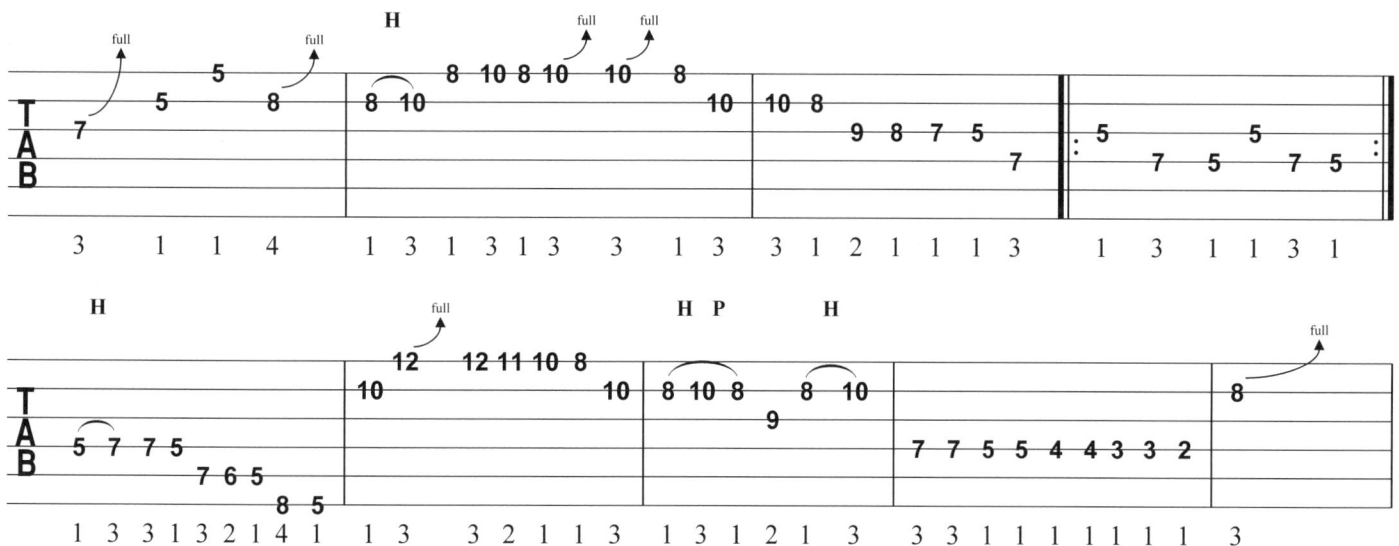

Creating a Great Blues Sound

Effect pedals (or stomp boxes) are often used to enhance or distort a guitar's tone. There are many different types of effects. The most popular effects used for blues guitar are overdrive, distortion, chorus, delay, reverb and wah wah. Below are a few of the most common ones. Take a trip to your local music store and try out a variety of effect pedals to hear which ones sound good to you.

Overdrive Pedal

A distortion or overdrive pedal simulates the sound of the guitar's signal being overdriven, giving it a fuzz tone. Overdrive can be used in different degrees. Light distortion will give the sound a warm, round or full tone. Using heavy distortion gives the guitar a heavy metal tone.

Chorus Pedal

A chorus pedal creates the sound of a few guitars played at once. A chorus doubles the original signal with a very slight delay, causing a wavy tone that simulates a chorus of guitars.

Wah Wah Pedal

A wah wah pedal is a foot activated pedal that you can "play" with your foot while playing the guitar. The pedal gets rocked back and forth by your foot and gives the guitar a talking, wah wah type sound. What a wah wah pedal actually does is sweep quickly back and forth between extreme bass and extreme treble driven by the movement of your foot.

Amplifier Gain

Turning up the gain knob on an amplifier overdrives the signal and creates distortion. Use small amounts of gain for a warm, thick tone. Using high gain will cause heavy distortion. Use the gain in conjunction with the amplifier's master volume control to set the desired tone and level of the sound.

Blues Riffs That Will Make Yo' Mama Scream!

Here's a collection of little riffs that will help you start building your own bag of tricks. These riffs use various positons of the A minor pentatonic scales, and incorporate all of the techniques we've covered so far. You can play all of these riffs at different speeds, with or without a shuffle feel, starting on any beat you choose. Any one of these is a good choice when soloing and improvising. Try coming up with some of your own variations.

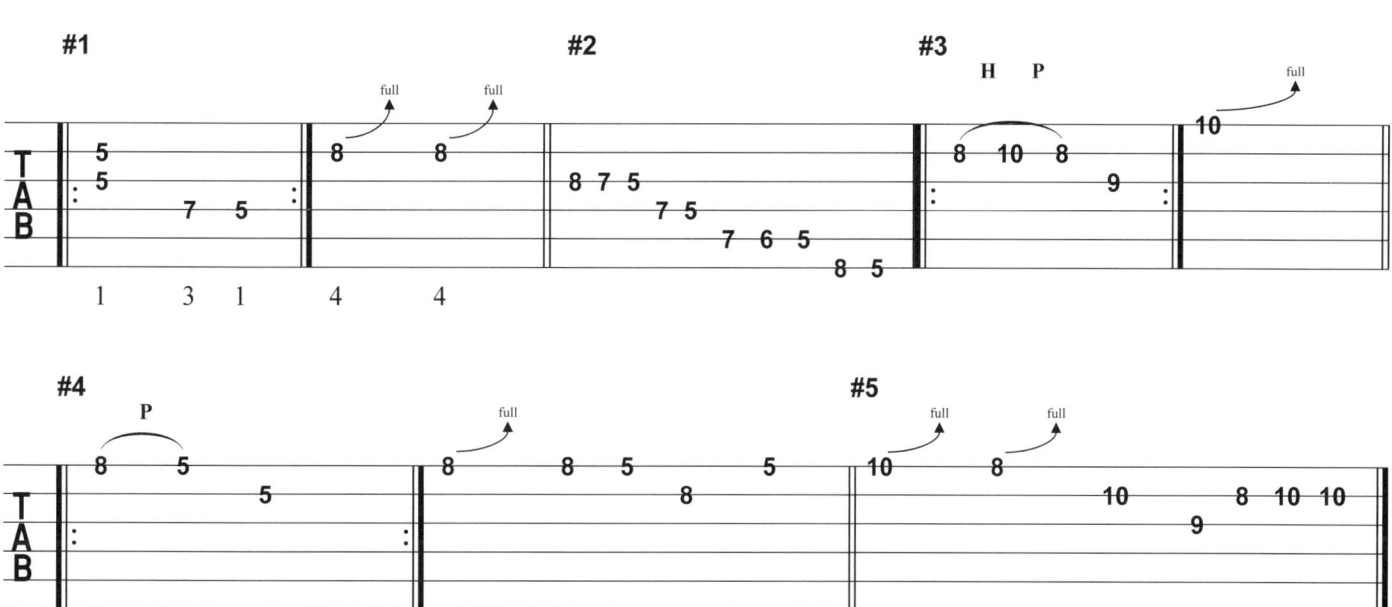

Quick Quote!

"I have heartaches, I have blues. No matter what you got, the blues is there. 'Cause that's all I know - the blues. And I can sing the blues so deep until you can have this room full of money and I can give you the blues."

- John Lee Hooker

Shuffle Blues Rhythm

This progression incorporates chords and single notes to make up the rhythm. This standard blues rhythm is in A and uses a I - IV - V progression. Practice along with the backing track to get the timing and the shuffle feel.

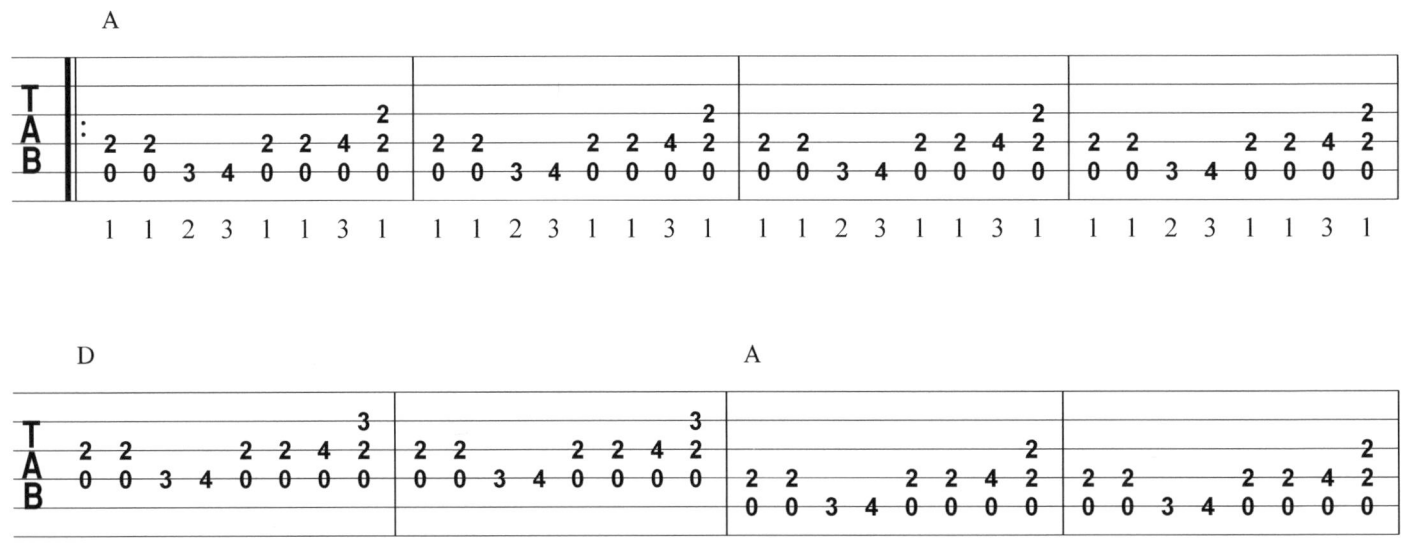

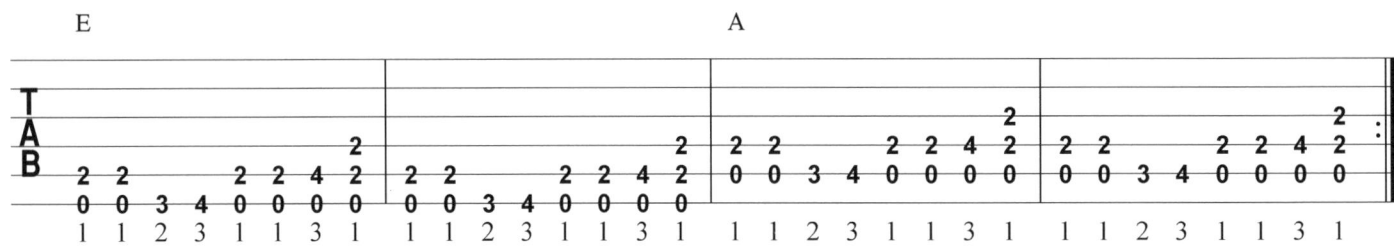

Complete Blues Lead

Here's a solo that uses all of the previous lead techniques in various positions on the neck. In the 11th measure, there's an example of a bend and release: after bending the note, gradually release the bend to the note's original pitch.

Download the backing track from RockHouseMethod.com and practice playing along with the band. The chord names above the tab staff are there for a reference to show you where the changes are.

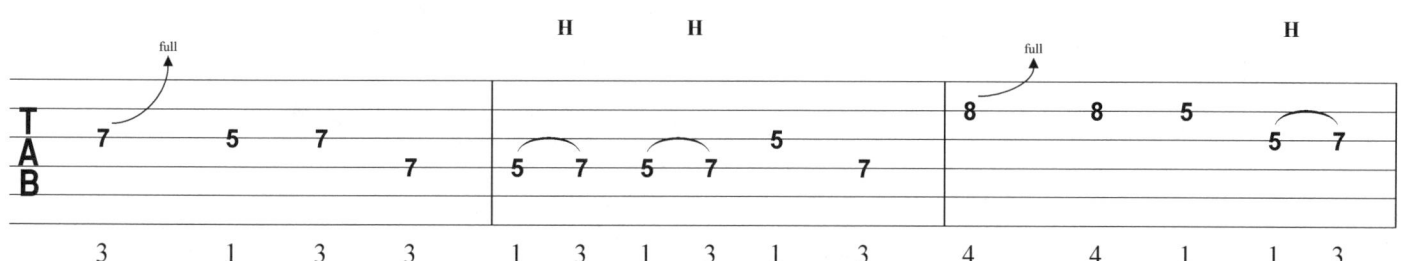

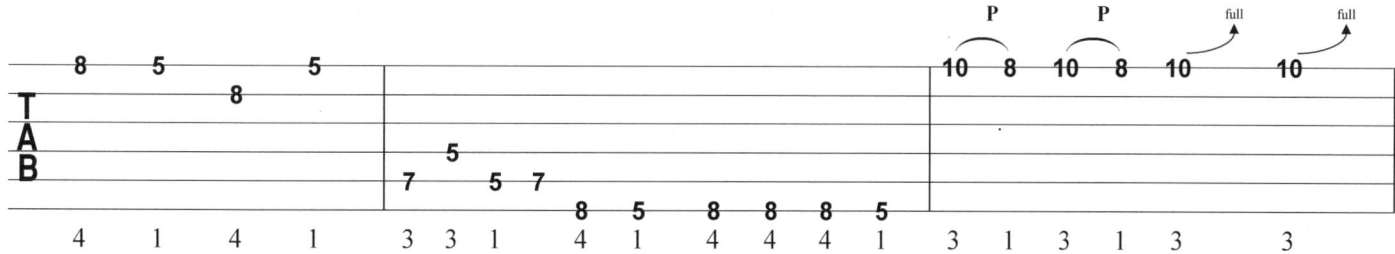

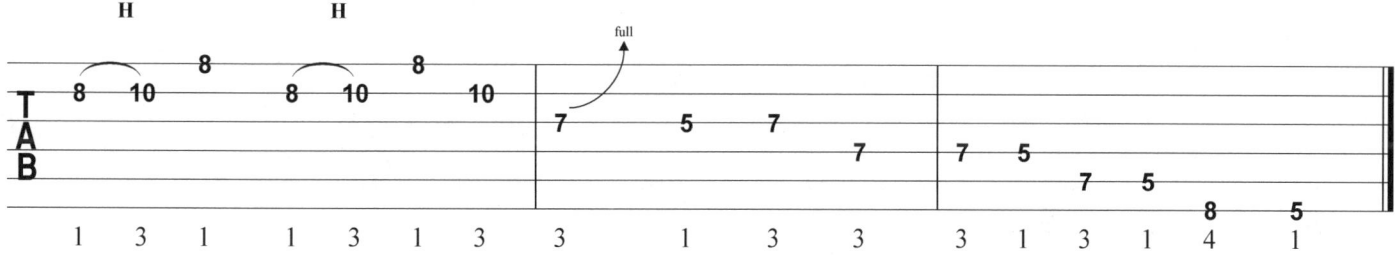

Blues

Intermediate

Blues Scales
Key of "E"

Program 2

The blues scale is a slight variation of the minor pentatonic scale. It contains one extra note between the 4th and 5th steps of the scale, called a passing tone. This particular passing tone is the flatted fifth of the scale, also known as the blues tri-tone. Using the blues tri-tone adds color and character to solos and riffs. This note is a chromatic passing tone because it passes from the 4th to the 5th steps of the scale in chromatic half steps. Passing tones are used to connect from note to note within a phrase and are generally not held for long durations.

The following five scale positions of the E blues scale are the same as the E minor pentatonic scale with the addition of the blues tri-tone. The notes in black in the scale diagrams indicate where the blues tri-tones are played. Practice and memorize the E blues scale positions; we'll be using these scales to play solos in many of the following sections.

The notes within the black circles represent the blues tri-tone.

1st Position

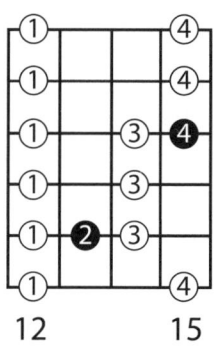
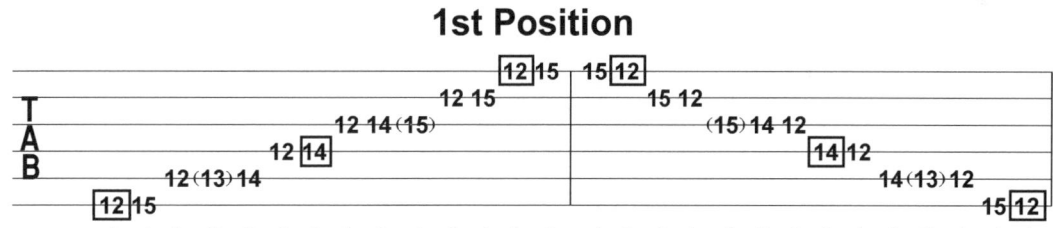

2nd Position

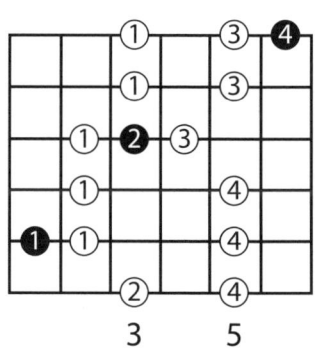
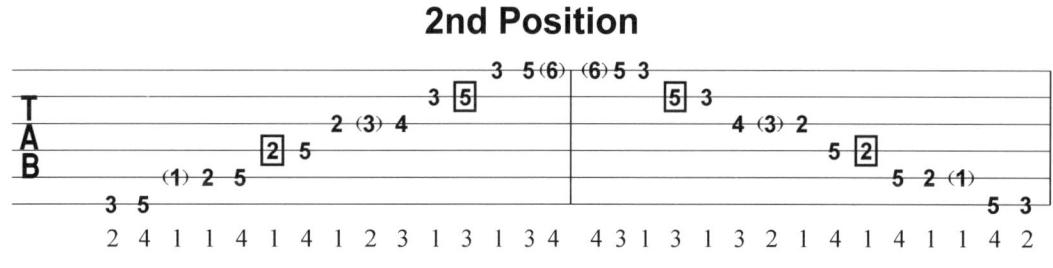

3rd Position

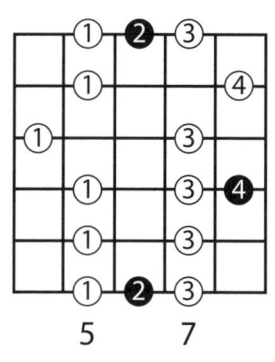
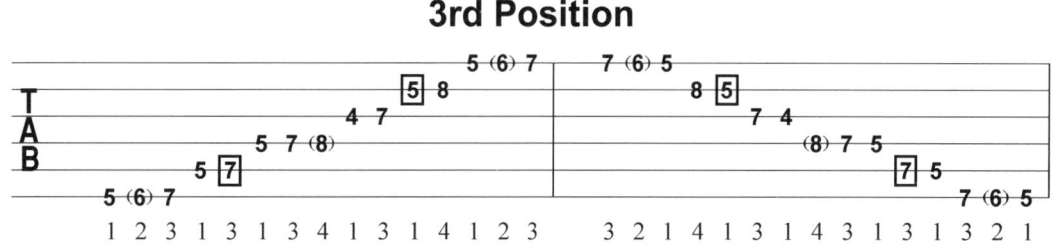

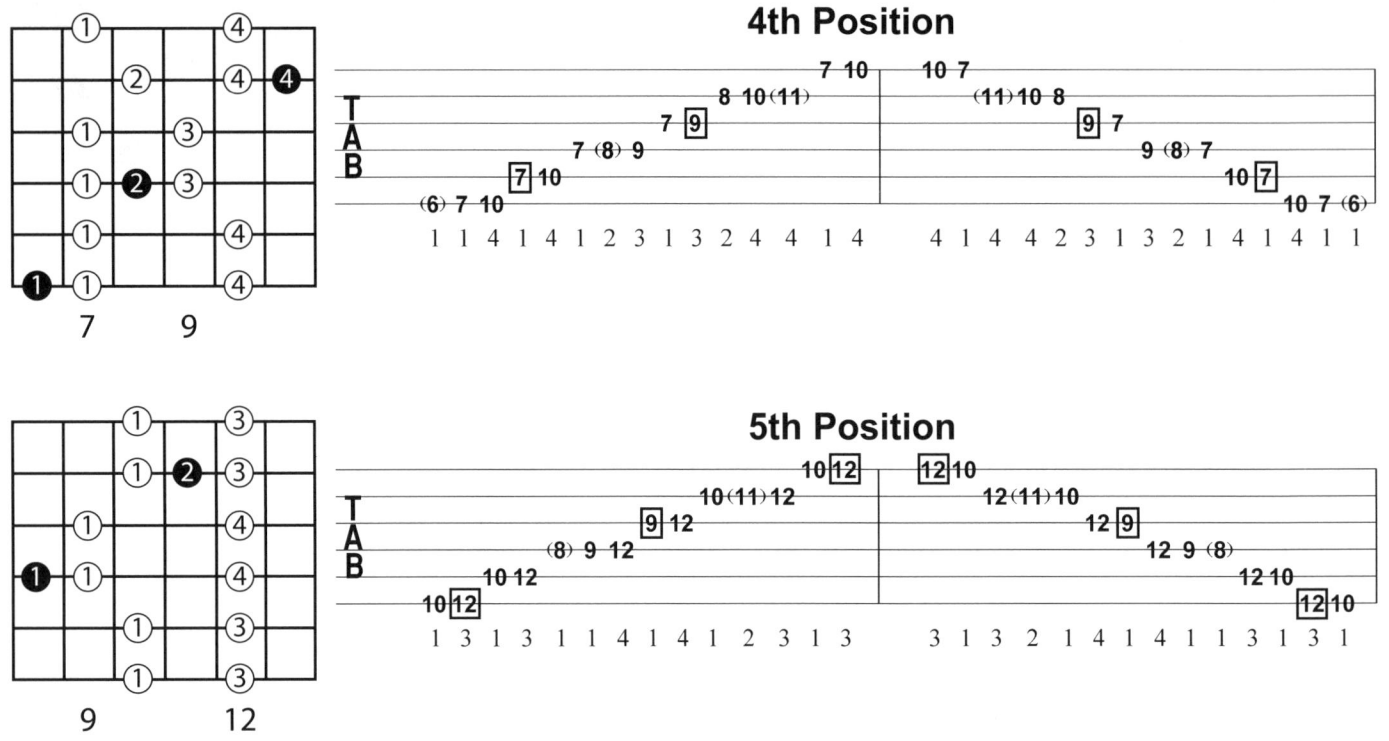

The Open Position "E" Blues Scale

The 1st position of the E blues scale can also be transposed one octave lower and played in open position. This particular scale position is used often in blues music. Playing in open position makes hammer ons, pull offs and trills very easy to perform, making this particular scale a favorite for many guitarists. To play any scale position an octave higher or lower, move the scale pattern 12 frets in the appropriate direction.

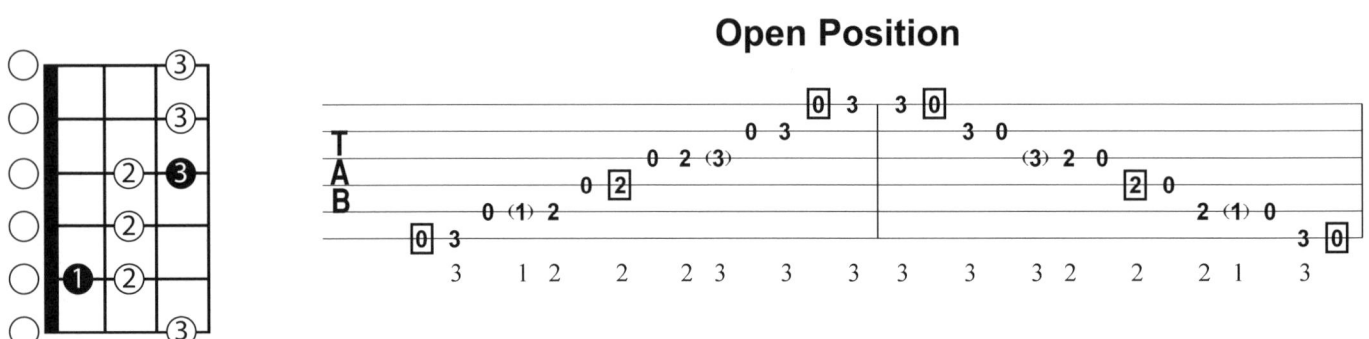

"E" Blues Scale Fretboard Diagram

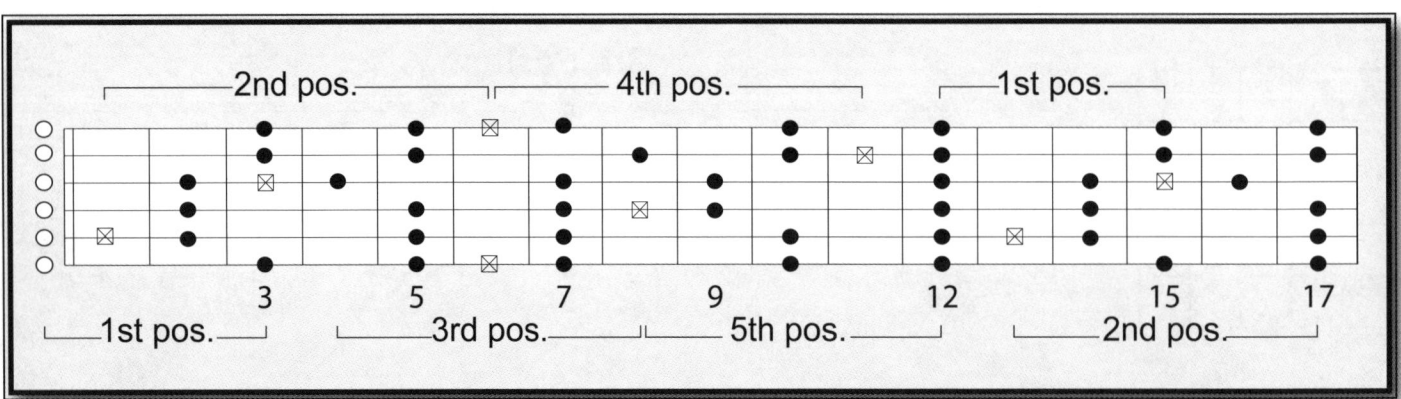

Open String Blues Rhtyhm in "E"

The following rhythm is a standard I - IV - V progression in E with a shuffle feel. The last two measure phrase is a turnaround (a riff that brings you back around to the beginning of the progression). The riff should be played using alternate picking; let the notes ring out together. This particular turnaround uses a descending chromatic riff leading back to the V (five) chord, B. Practice the rhythm along with the backing track, then improvise and solo over it using the E blues scale in various positions.

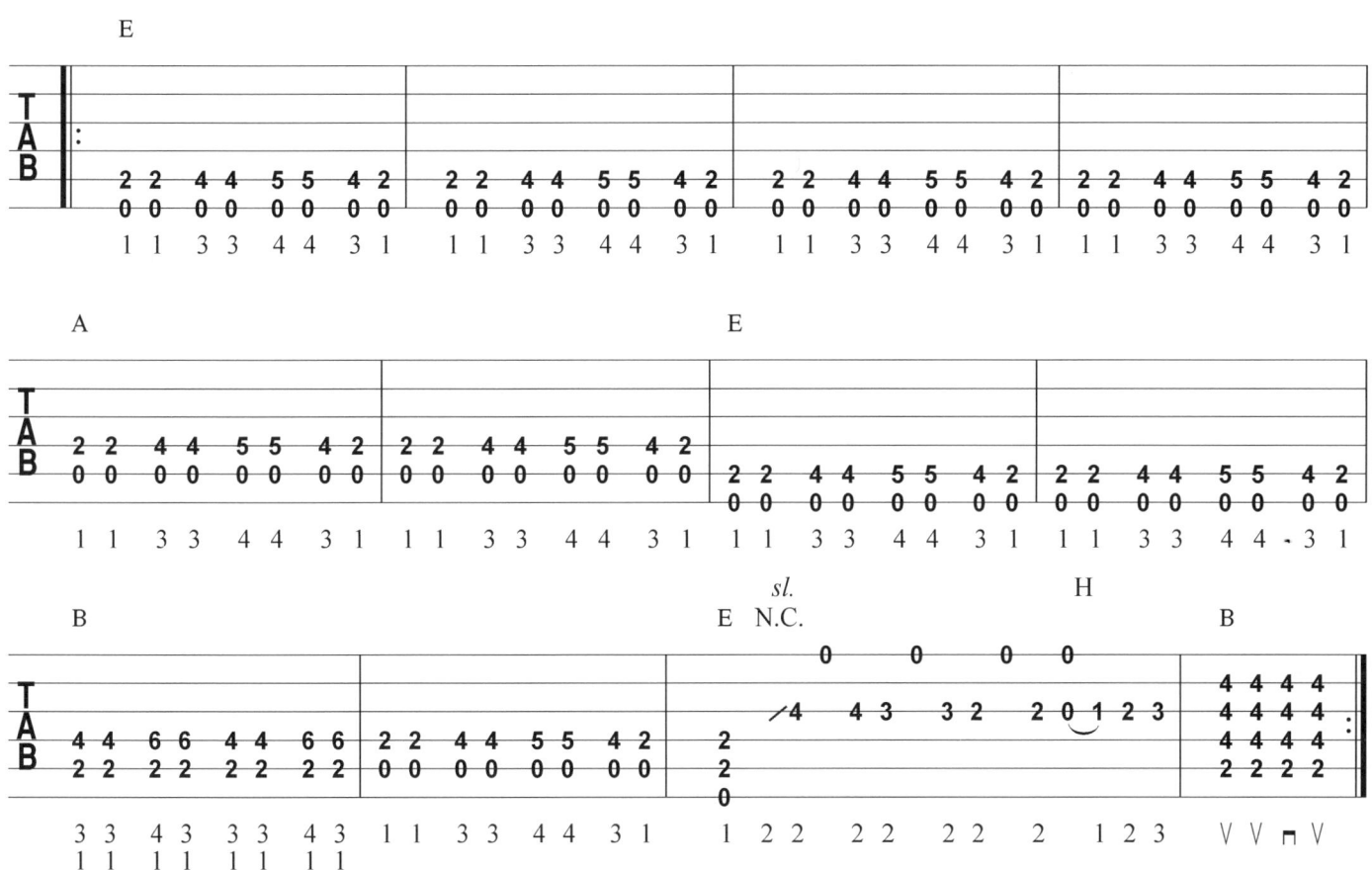

Quick Quote!

"If they played more blues, people would just get it - they try to hold it back but just about can't hold it back now because the blues is really going."

- John Lee Hooker

Blues Lead in "E"

Here's an example of a blues lead that can be played over the Open String Blues Rhythm in E from earlier in this section. Listen to the backing track to get the rhythm and the phrasing. This solo incorporates many different types of bends as well as hammer ons, pull offs, and slides.

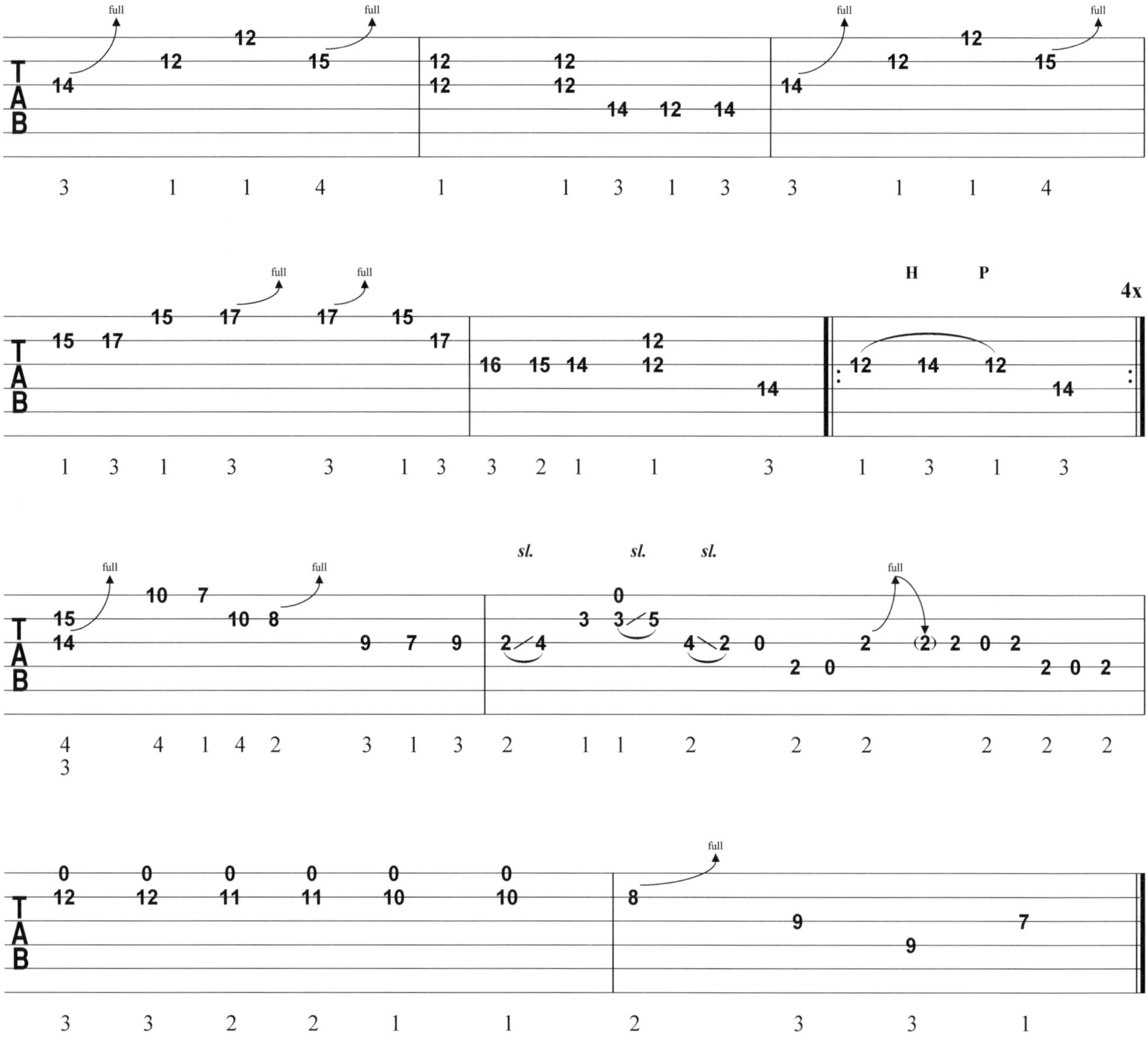

Bar Chords

Let's begin this section by expanding your chord vocabulary. The following full barre chords contain no open strings, so they are moveable chords; you can transpose them to any fret. After mastering these chords, you'll be able to play in any key and position on the guitar.

6th String Bar Chords

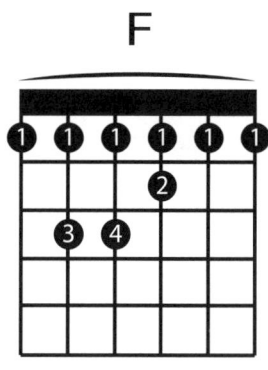

Notice that the lowest note of the chord is F, the root note. Using the musical alphabet, you can move barre chords up the neck and change them to any chord in the scale. Use the following chart to find any chord along the 6th string by moving the F chord. The name of the chord will change depending on which fret you move the chord to. The Fm chord at the bottom of this page will also be movable and will change names following the same chart. For example the Fm chord moved to the 5th nfret would ba an Am chord.

Name -	F	F#	G	G#	A	A#	B	C	C#	D	D#	E
Fret -	1	2	3	4	5	6	7	8	9	10	11	12

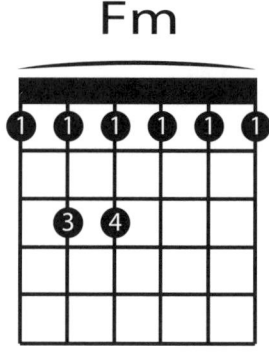

41

F7

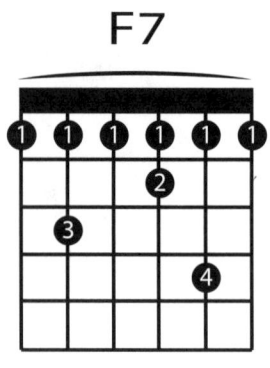

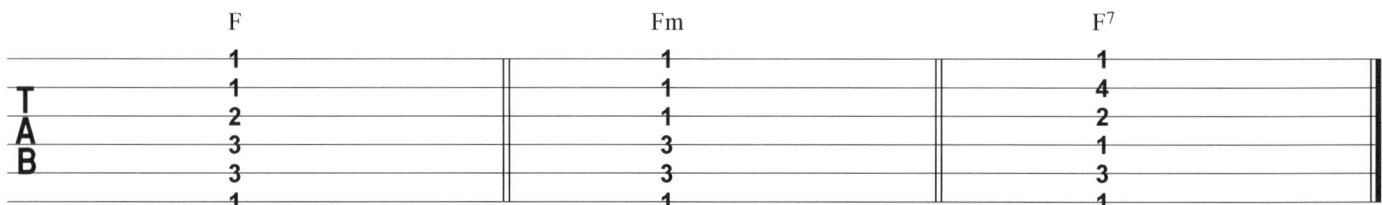

5th String Bar Chords

The Bb major barre chord is played at the 1st fret with the root note on the 5th string. This chord has a third finger barre. Make sure the 1st and 6th strings are muted and not strummed. Use the chart below to transpose this chord to any other fret along the 5th string.

Bb

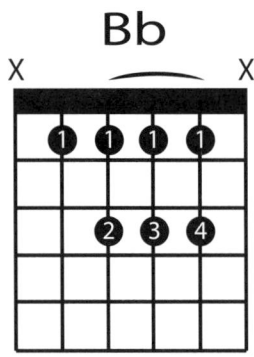

Name -	Bb	B	C	C#	D	D#	E	F	F#	G	G#	A
Fret -	1	2	3	4	5	6	7	8	9	10	11	12

The Bbm and Bb7 barre chords are played using a first finger bar. Once you have them mastered, try transposing both chords to other frets using the 5th string chart on the previous page.

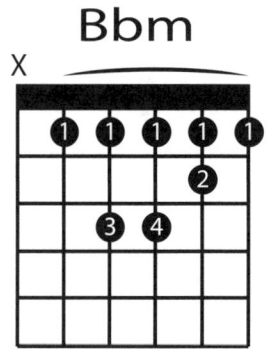

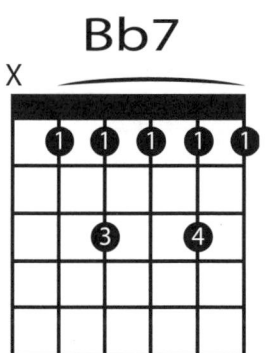

Quick Quote!

"It is from the blues that all that may be called American music derives its most distinctive character. "

- James Weldon Johnson

12 Bar Blues Progression

12-bar blues is a progression based on the I - IV - V chords that is 12 measures long. Most blues music is made up of 12-bar blues progressions; 12 measures of music that repeat throughout the song. This particular example combines barre chords and single notes in the key of A. The single notes at the end of each measure are played with the first and third fingers in the same positon as each chord. Play along with the backing track to get the shuffle feel.

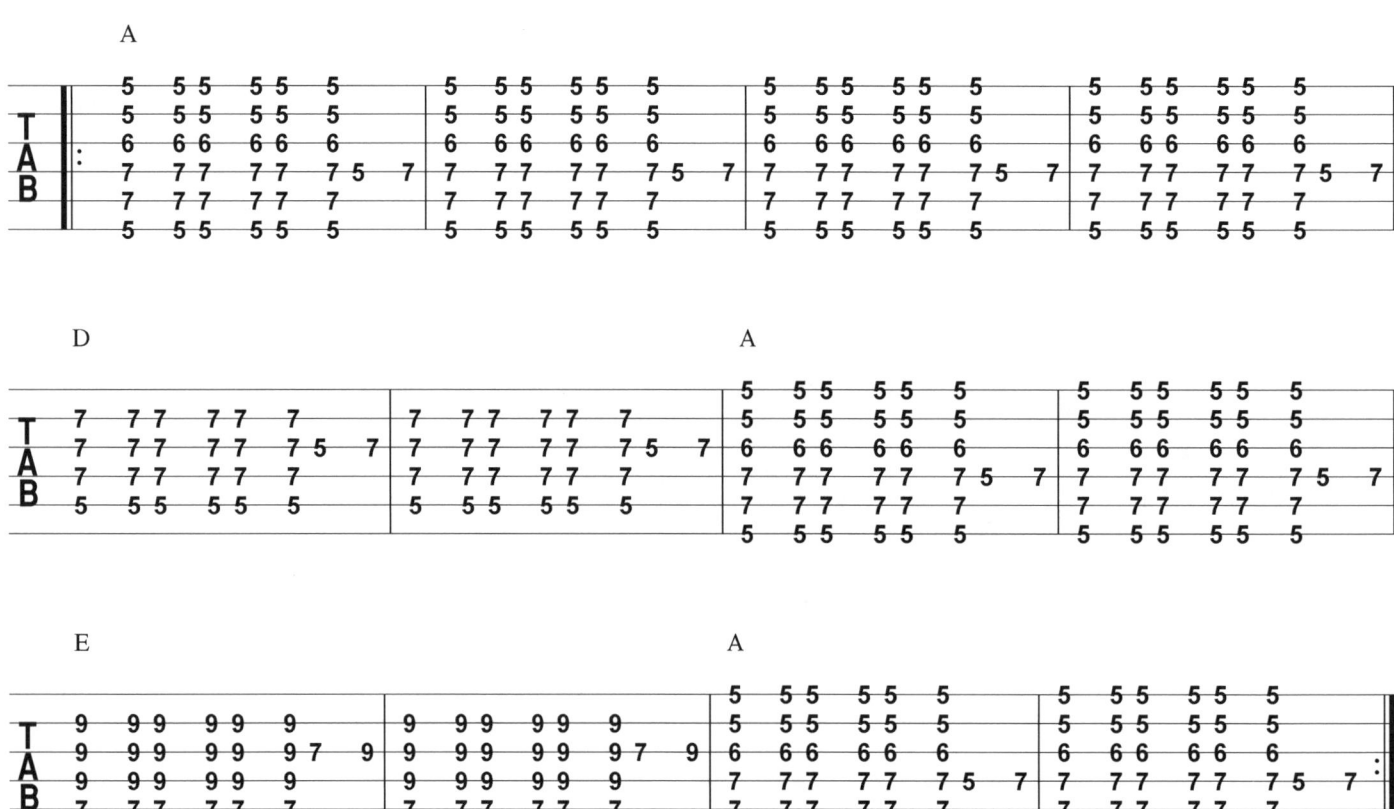

12 Bar Theory

Let's discuss the basic theory behind the 12 bar blues form. As we said before the 12 bar progression is commonly used in blues music. This progression is 12 bars or measures consisting of only the I, IV, and V chords of a given key. To determine which chords they are let's look at the notes of a one octave C Major Scale:

C Major Scale – C D E F G A B C

Now let's add numeric degrees to the scale:

C	D	E	F	G	A	B	C
I	II	III	IV	V	VI	VII	I

If you look at the diagram above you will notice that the C is I, F is the IV, and G is the V. Commonly in blues we would take these three degrees and form Dominant 7th chords from them which would give us the C7, F7, and G7 Chords. However, if you want a Major or minor Blues, you could substitute either major or minor chords for these.

Now let's look at two commonly used forms of the 12 bar blues progression. One is called "Slow Changes" and the other is called "Fast Changes." The difference between slow and fast changes is the second measure. Slow changes is when the I chord is played for the first four measures. Fast changes is when the IV chord is played in place of the I chord in the second measure. Both of these have a distinct sound that is heard commonly in both Blues and Rock music.

12 Bar "Slow Changes"

C7	C7	C7	C7
F7	F7	C7	C7
G7	F7	C7	G7

12 Bar "Fast Changes"

C7	F7	C7	C7
F7	F7	C7	C7
G7	F7	C7	G7

Skipping Strings - 3rds & 5ths

This is another blues technique using the pick and finger method. When fretting the notes, use your second finger for all of the notes along the 3rd string. Alternate between your pick and middle finger to pluck the notes. The riff is shown ascending and then descending. Try this technique at different speeds and in different rhythms.

Example 1

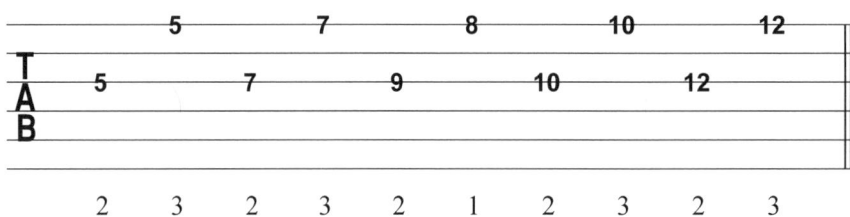

Example 2

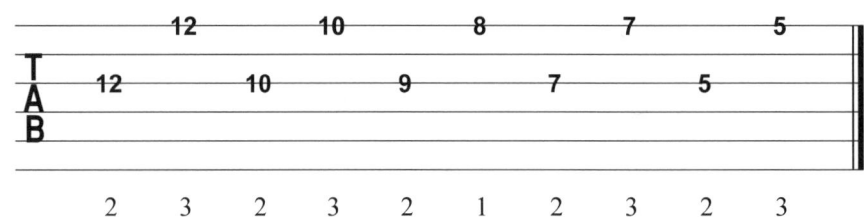

Quick Quote!

"It was stumbling on to really the bible of the blues, you know, and a very powerful drug to be introduced to us and I absorbed it totally, and it changed my complete outlook on music."

- Eric Clapton

Blues Single Note Riff Rhythm

Here's a shuffle rhythm guitar progression consisting of all single notes. This pattern is a good example of a riff. The riff is outlined in the first measure. As the progression follows a 12-bar blues, the riff is transposed to each new chord. This example is also based around a I - IV - V chord change in the key of D (D - G - A). Once you have this progression down, try to create some of your own single note riff rhythms.

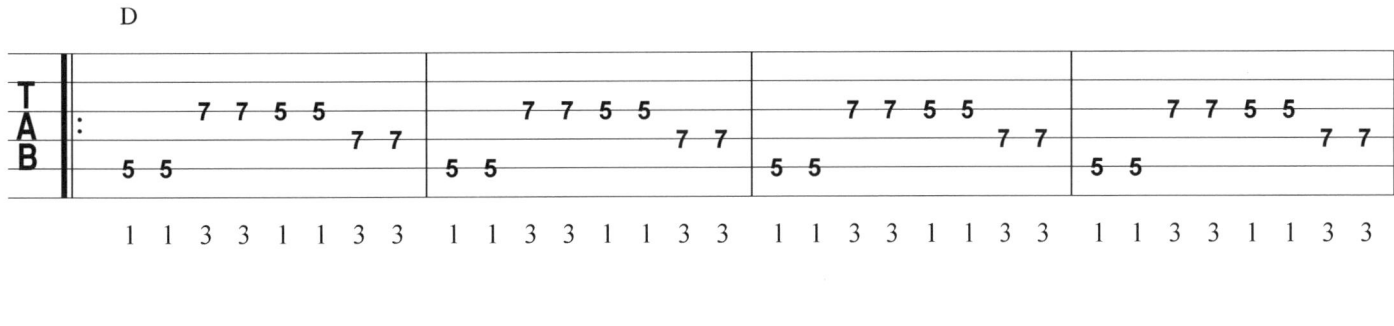

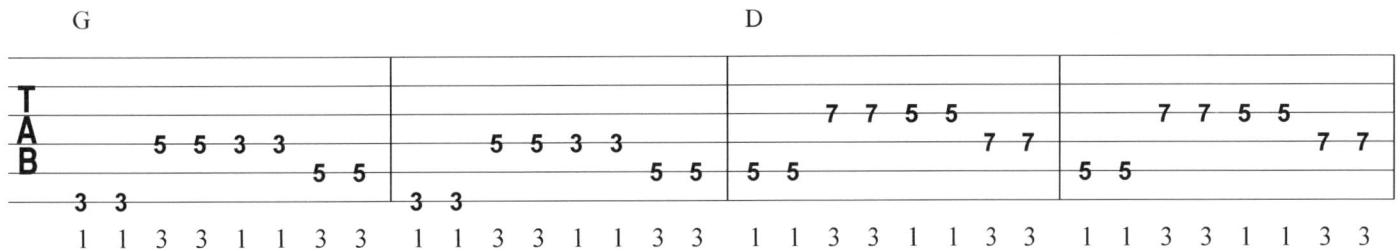

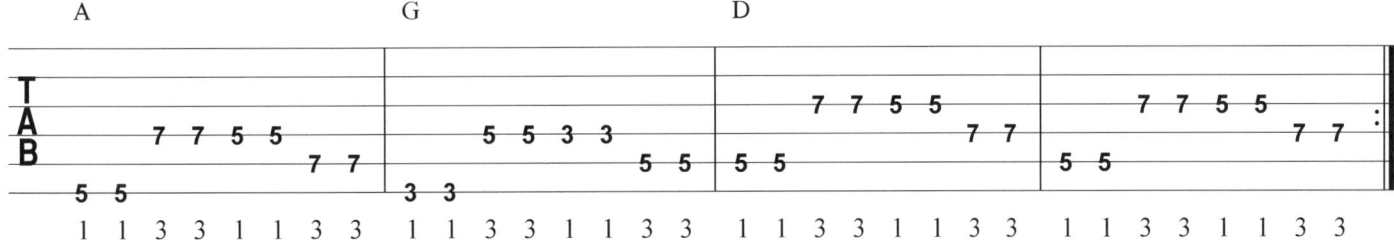

Slides & Vibrato

Slides

In the following example, slide from note to note without lifting your finger off the fretboard. The "*sl.*" above the staff indicates a slide and the line between the notes shows the direction of the slide (up or down the neck). If there is a slur connecting two or more notes, pick only the first note and slide directly to the next without picking. You can perform slides using any finger, but you'll probably use first and third finger slides more often. This exercise is played using the 1st position A minor pentatonic scale. After you get this down, try using the slide technique in other positions as well.

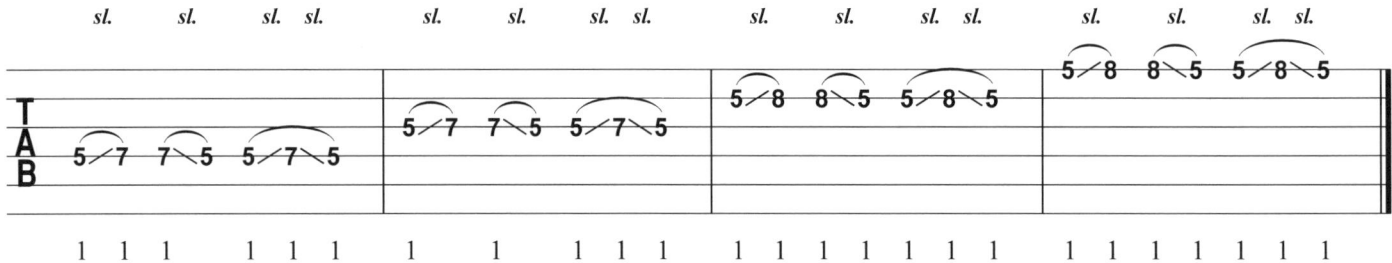

Vibrato

Vibrato is the small, fast shaking of a note. Vibrato is indicated by a squiggly line above the staff, extending out from a note. While sustaining a note, shake your finger slightly and "dig in" to the note to slightly vibrate the pitch and give it more expression. Vibrato can also be applied while bending.

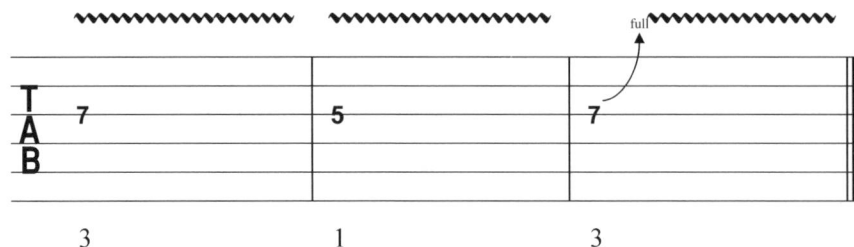

Rockin' the Blues

This progression incorporates dead strums which are performed by muting the strings with your left hand and strumming the muted strings. These muted notes are shown using x's on the tab staff. Pay attention to the picking symbols below the staff that show you when to up-strum or down-strum. This particular example places dead strums between most of the normal strums, giving the progression more of percussive sound and a rock feel. This progression is also played with a shuffle feel.

```
    A                                               C           D
T|--2---2---X---2---X---2---X---2---|--X---2--2---2---5---5---7---7--|
A|--2---2---X---2---X---2---X---2---|--X---2--2---2---5---5---7---7--|
B|--2---2---X---2---X---2---X---2---|--X---2--2---2---5---5---7---7--|
 |--0---0---X---0---X---0---X---0---|--X---0--0---0---3---3---5---5--|

    ⊓   V   ⊓   V   ⊓   V   ⊓   V      ⊓   V ⊓ V   ⊓   V   ⊓   V
```

Quick Quote!

> "The Blues are the true facts of life expressed in words and song, inspiration, feeling, and understanding."
>
> - Willie Dixon

Using the Metronome to Practice

As you progress as a guitarist you can use the metronome in your daily practice to help keep a steady rhythm and gauge your progress. Here are a few metronome practice tips that will help you use this tool effectively.

1. When starting to learn a new song set the metronome at a slow tempo where you can play the entire piece through without making mistakes.

2. Gradually build your speed by increasing the BPM (beats per minute) on the metronome a few numbers each day.

3. As you play with the metronome try not to focus on it too much. Sense the feel of the click and concentrate on the song you are playing.

Blues Riffs That Will Make Yo' Mama Scream! Part 2

These riffs incorporate all of the lead techniques over several positions of the Am pentatonic scale. The last riff uses a double stop slide (sliding two notes at once). After mastering these riffs, try transposing them to other keys and positions on the fretboard and also try to create your own Blues riffs using the Minor Pentatonic Scales.

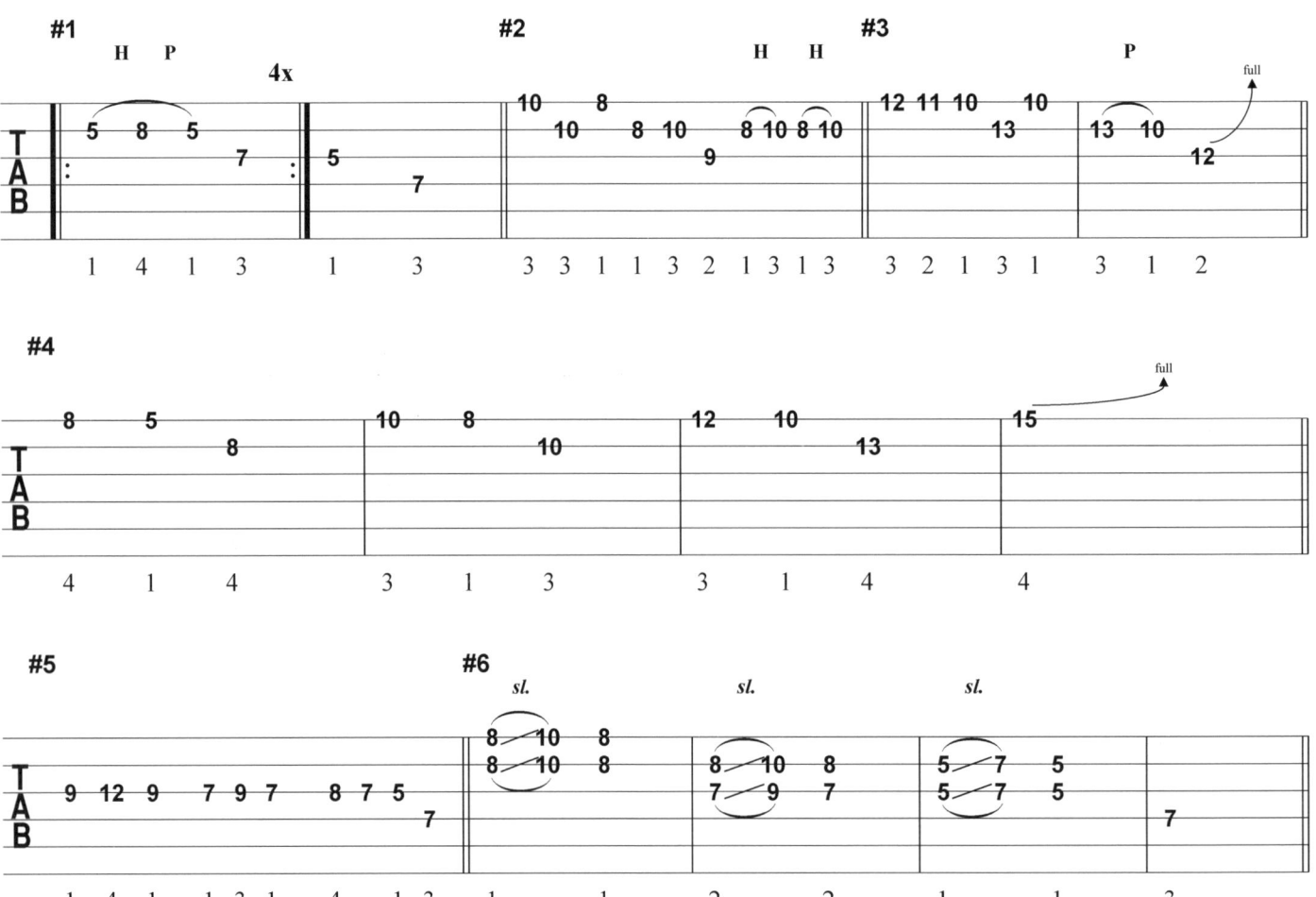

The BB Box

The BB Box is a section of the minor pentatonic scale that overlaps the 1st and 2nd positions. The name refers to the great B.B. King because he bases a lot of his soloing around this part of the scale. The following fretboard diagram indicates which notes are in the BB Box (in the key of Am) using solid black dots. The open circles show the minor pentatonic scale notes in the surrounding positions. Refer to the tab staff below the diagram for the proper fingering.

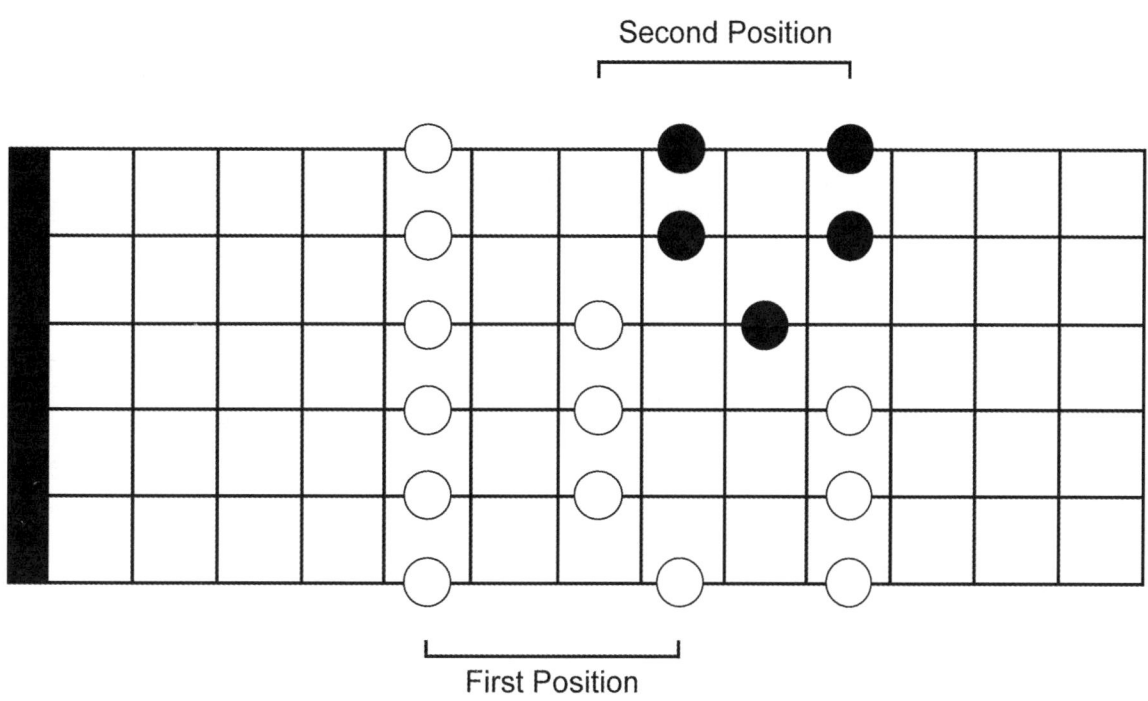

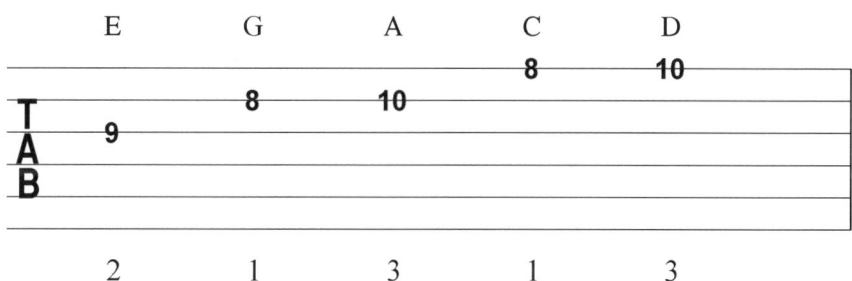

Above each tab number is its note name. Notice that A (the root note) is in between the other notes of the scale. The B.B. Box takes the five notes of the minor pentatonic scale and puts the root note in the middle. This position allows you to play around the root note, playing a few notes up or a few notes down from it. This is also the way many blues singers arrange their vocal melodies. The B.B. Box is great for soloing off the vocal melody or for trading riffs back and forth with the singer.

51

Open Chord Blues Smokin' Rhythm

The following progression uses some new open chord variations and suspensions. The chord diagrams show the fingerings for the chords used in this exercise. Notice that the fingering for the Em chord has been varied slightly in order to make it easier to change from chord to chord. Play along with the backing track and get the rhythm down. After you've learned the rhythm part, you can transpose the minor pentatonic scale positions to Em and solo over it. The five positions of the E minor pentatonic scale are exactly the same as the E blues scales only without the blues tri-tone. When creating your solos, use bends, hammer-ons, pull-offs, slides and vibrato to add personal expression to your playing.

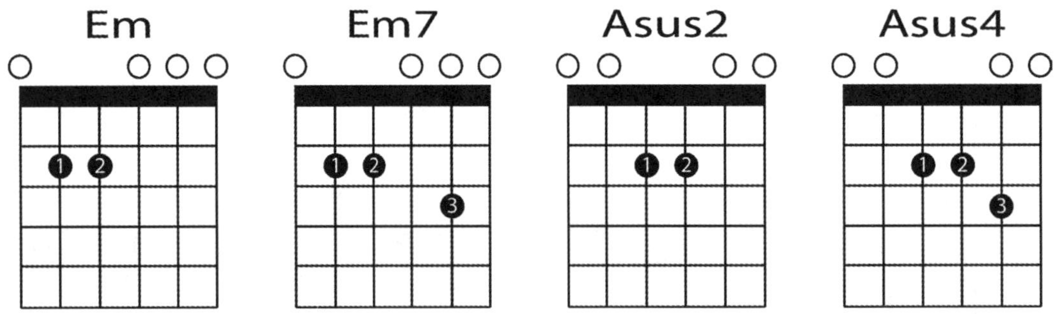

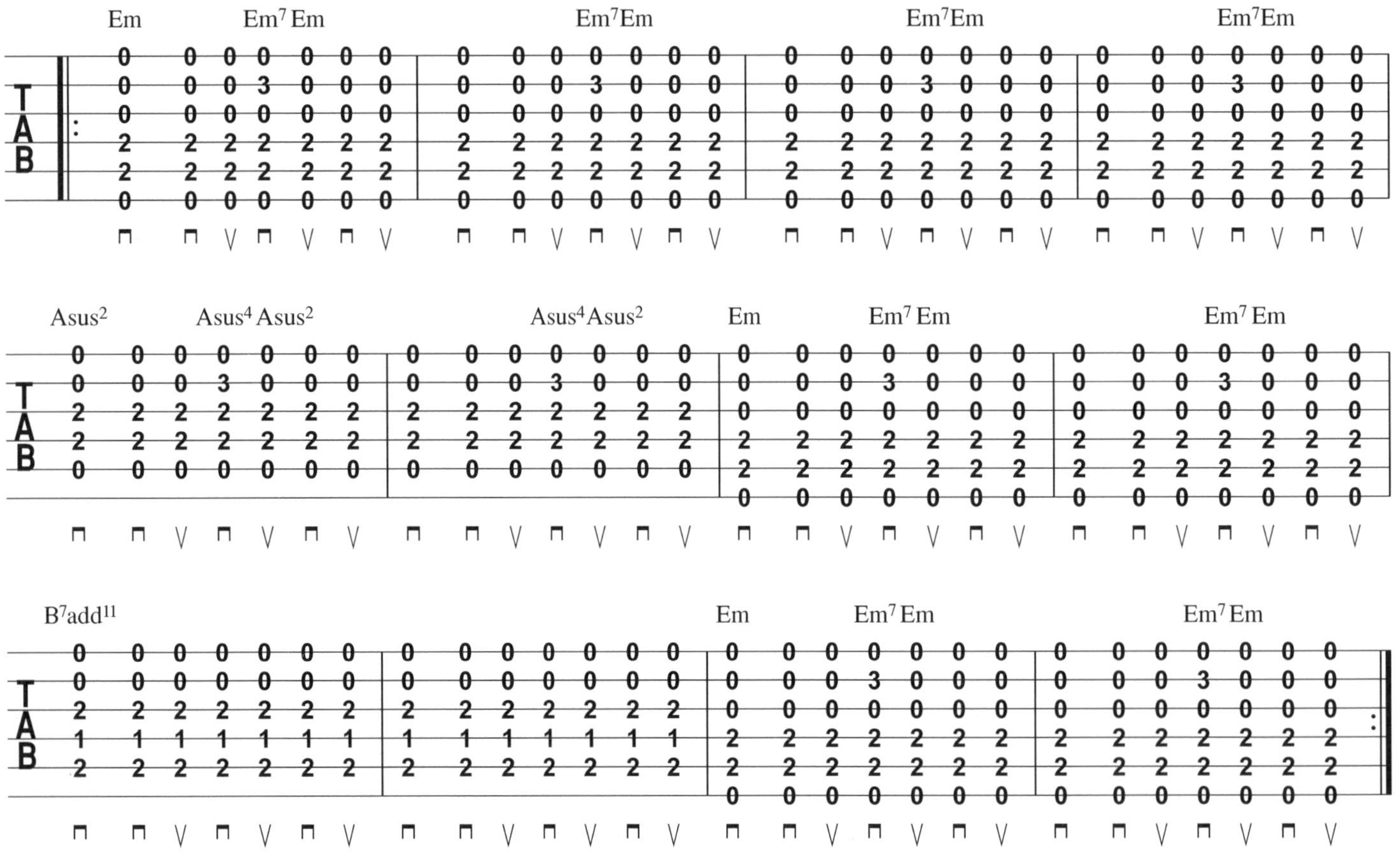

Blues

Advanced

Bonus Lessons

Major Pentatonic Scales
Key of "C"

The key of C major is the relative major to the key of A minor. A minor and C major are relative keys because they both contain the same notes. When playing in A minor, A is the root note; when playing in C major, C is the root note. The following five scale positions are the exact same scale fingerings as the A minor pentatonic scales from Chapter 2, however the root note is now going to be C. The root notes are circled on the tab staff, and are shown as open dots on the scale diagrams. Memorize where the root notes are in every scale position in order to solo in C major.

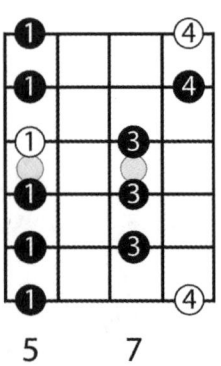
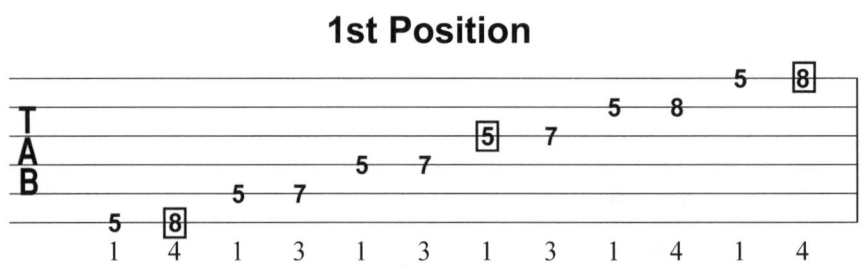

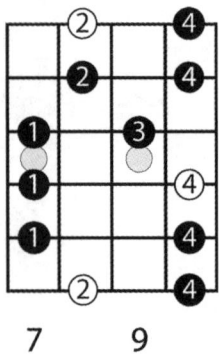
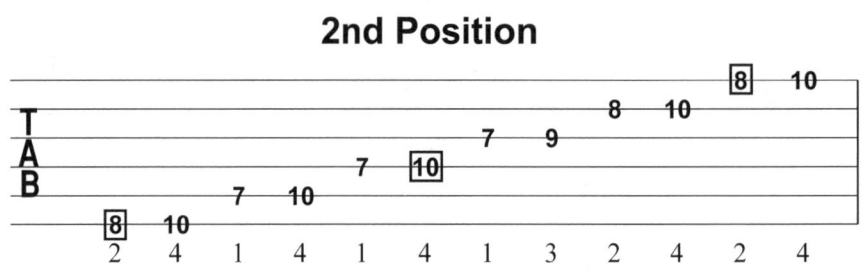

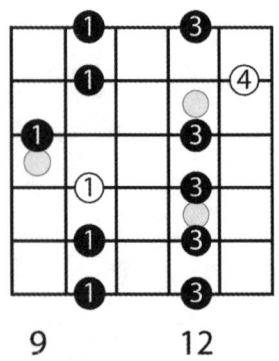
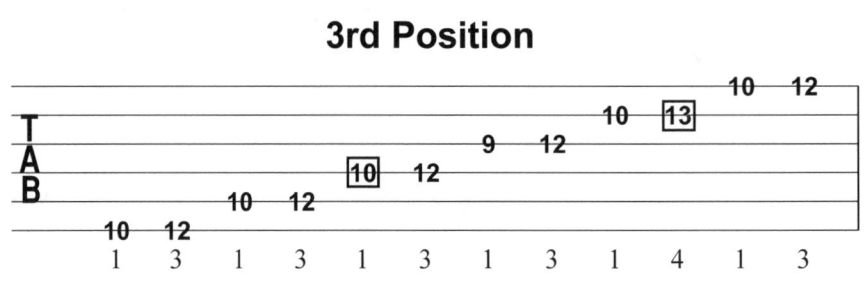

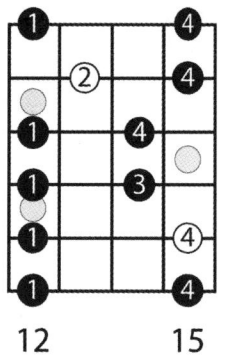

12   15

4th Position

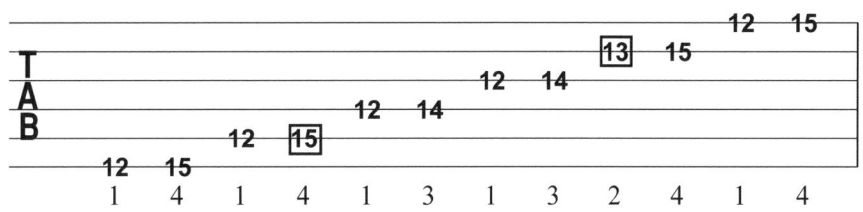

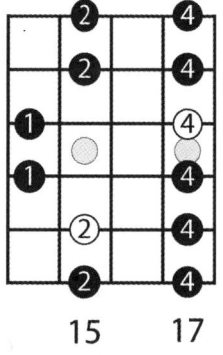

15   17

5th Position

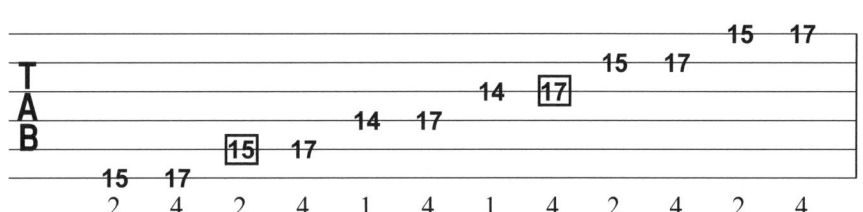

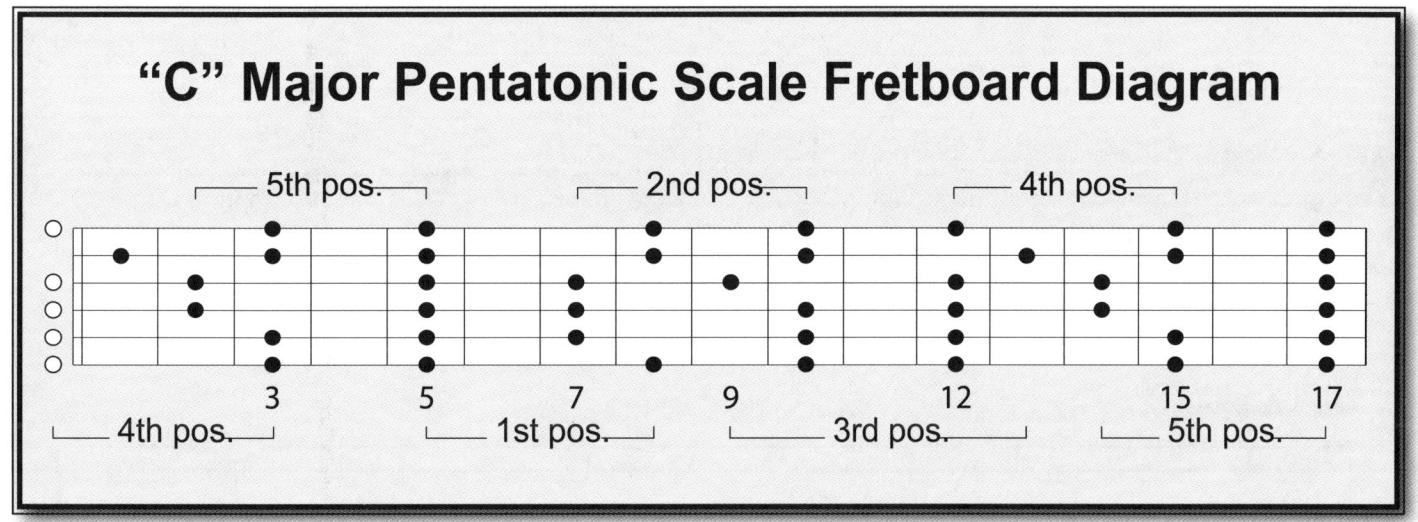

"C" Fast Blues

This rhythm is a fast I - IV - V shuffle in C major. After learning this rhythm, you can solo along with the backing track using the C major pentatonic scales. The fingering is shown under the first staff; use the same fingering for the rest of the progression. When performing the slides and double-stops, lean your second finger downward slightly to deaden the string that's in between the two notes being played.

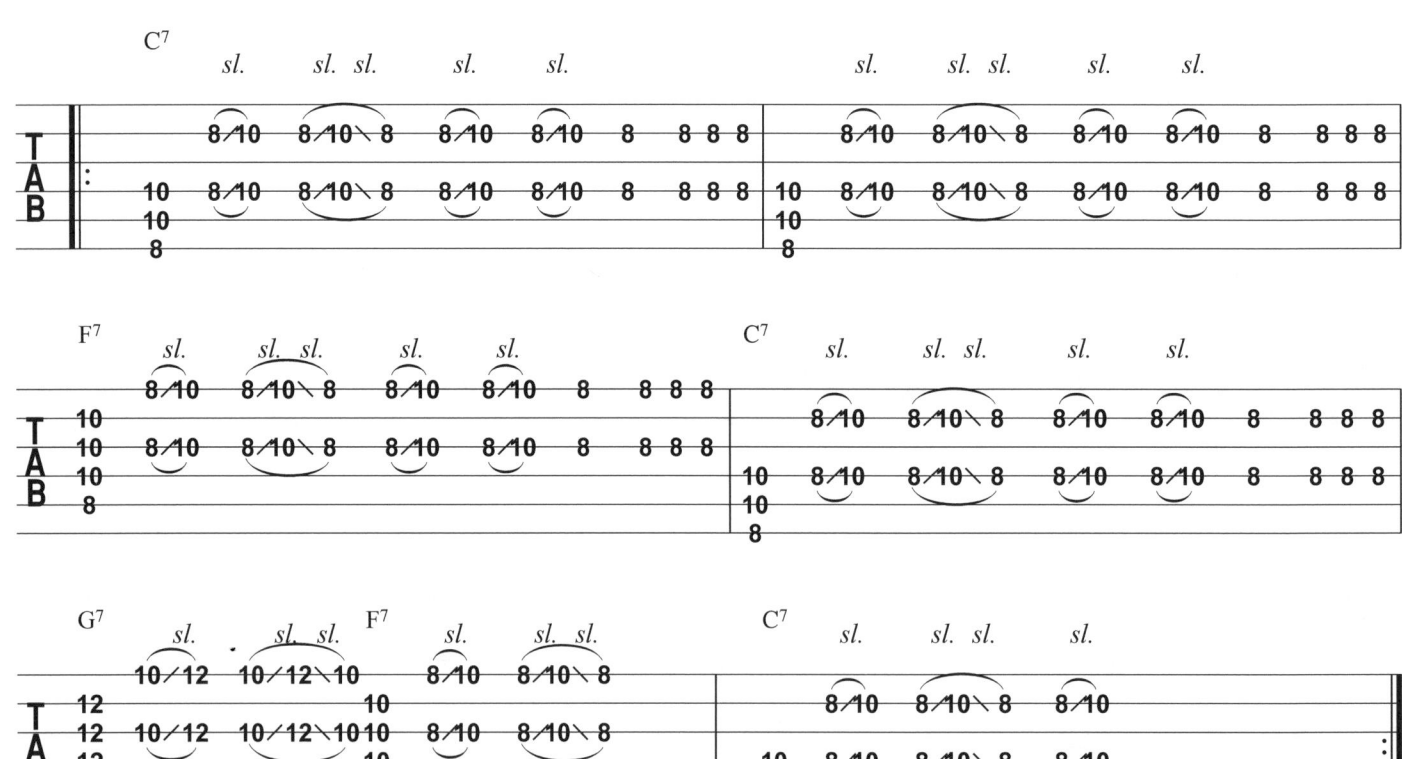

Quick Quote!

"Them pains, when blues pains grab you, you'll sing the blues right."

- Otis Rush

Combining Major & Minor Scales

You can create a call and response effect by switching back and forth between the major and minor keys while soloing. Compare the two scale positions below. Notice that the finger pattern is the same for both scales; the major starts at the 5th fret, the minor starts at the 8th fret. The difference is in the placement of the root notes. This forms an easy way for you to switch from major to minor just by moving the scale position three frets. To play a major pentatonic scale, move any of the minor pentatonic scale positions down three frets.

Try soloing over the Fast Blues in C from the previous section using both the major and minor pentatonics. You can solo for a few bars in major, then move three frets higher and solo in minor for a few bars to achieve a call and response effect. This is demonstrated on the DVD program to give you some ideas on how to use this technique.

"C" Major Pentatonic

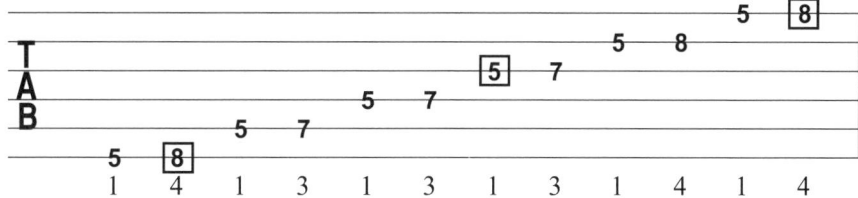

"C" Minor Pentatonic

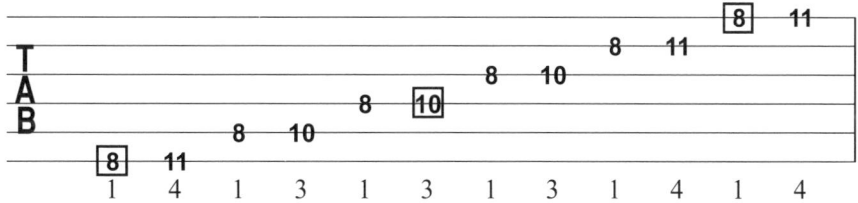

57

Improvisational Exercise

Many blues solos are created around the expansion of a main riff or phrase. You can take a simple, recognizable melody and keep coming back to it or play slight variations of it. This main theme gives the listener something to grasp on to in the same way as a chorus or hook does.

The melody below is shown in three different octaves on the guitar. Play over the same C major backing track and try working out a solo around this simple melody. You can play it anywhere within the progression; these themes work especially well when used in a turnaround. This technique is also demonstrated on the DVD. Once you understand the concept, try creating your own themes and melodies to build leads around.

Octave 1

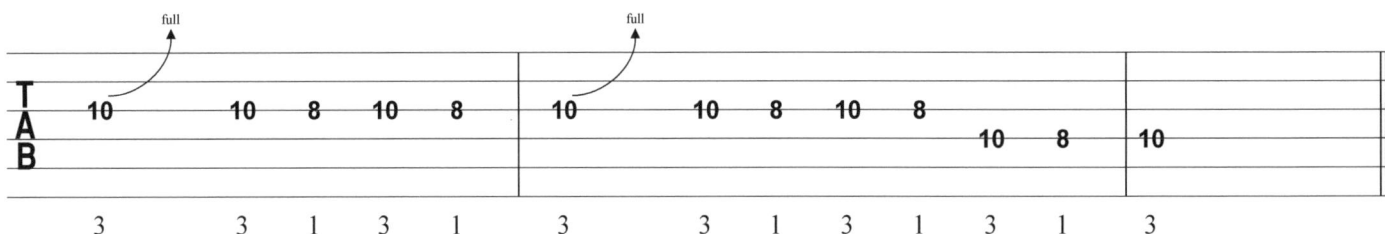

Octave 2

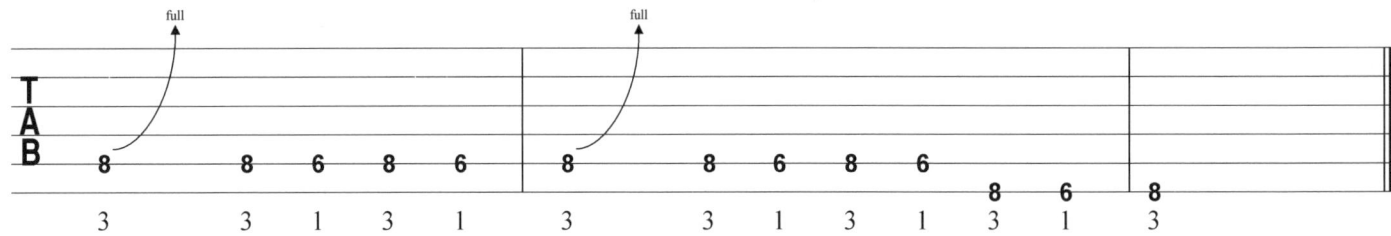

Octave 3

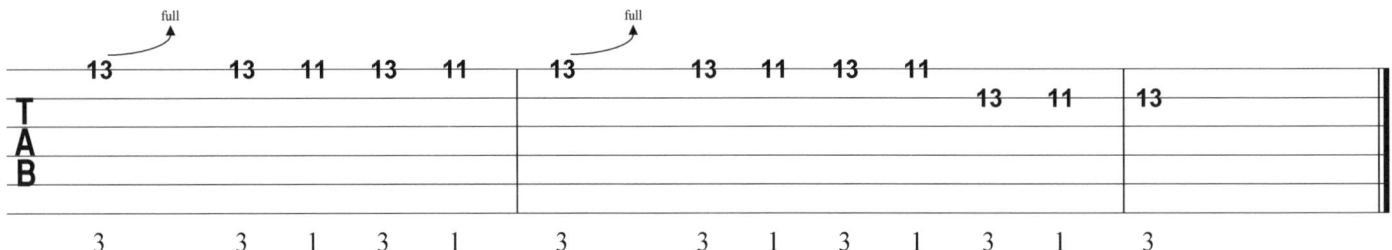

Advanced Bending Techniques

Half Step Bend

Half step bends are especially useful for soloing with blues scales. Train your ear to hear the difference between whole step and half step bends; eventually your fingers will instinctively know how much to bend the strings to achieve the correct pitches.

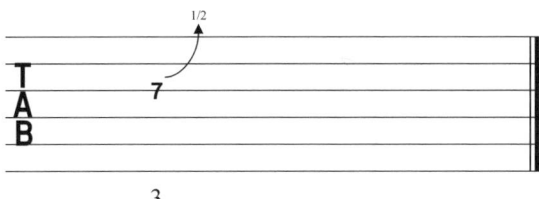

Ghost Bend

Ghost bends (sometimes referred to as pre-bends) are performed by bending the note to the proper pitch before striking the note. In this example, pre-bend the note a half step and then pick the note and gradually release the note to its original pitch.

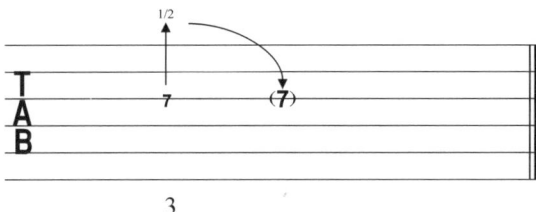

Double Pump Bend

You also bend and release the same note repeatedly without picking it again. The following example uses a bend-release-bend-release pattern. This technique can be used in a variety of ways.

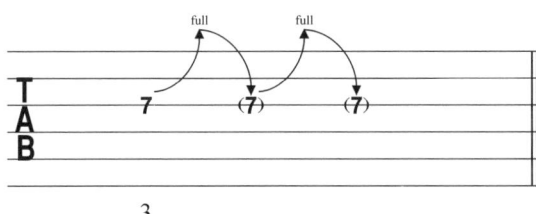

Scream Bend

To perform the following scream bend, pick both notes simultaneously and bend just the lower note up a whole step. Keep the higher note stationary and allow it to ring out along with the bend.

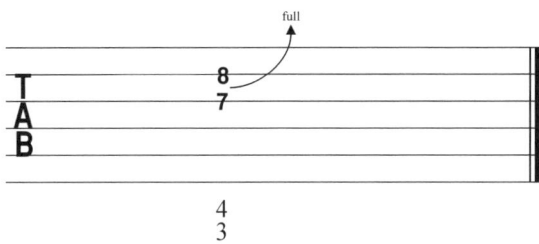

Bar Chord Review

Root 6 Bar Chords

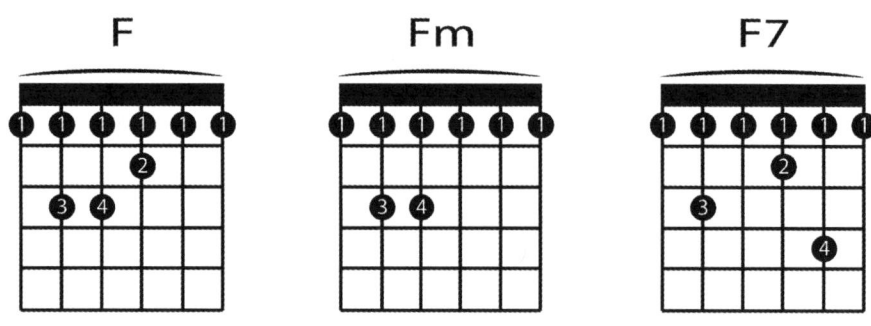

Root 5 Bar Chords

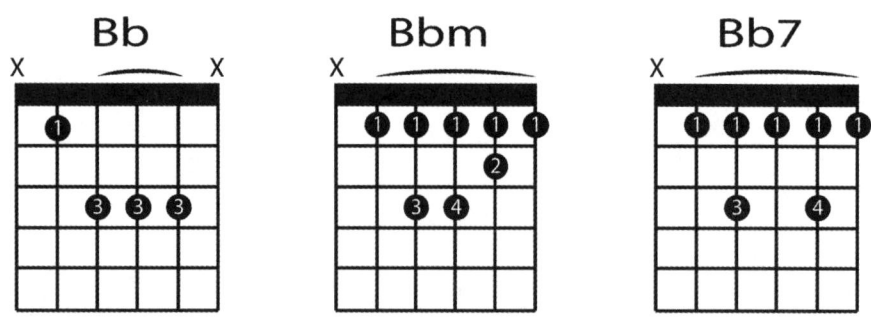

Name -	F	F#	G	G#	A	A#	B	C	C#	D	D#	E
Fret -	1	2	3	4	5	6	7	8	9	10	11	12
Name -	Bb	B	C	C#	D	D#	E	F	F#	G	G#	A

Rakes

A rake is a series of muted adjacent strings picked before a note. Pick downward across the strings in one sweeping motion while deadening them with your left hand. In this example, the x's represent the rake leading into the notes on the 1st string. Rakes are commonly used to accent a bend.

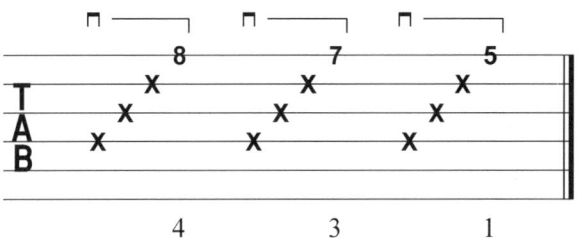

Blues Riffs That Will Make Yo' Mama Scream! Part 3

These riffs incorporate all of the lead techniques over several positions of the Em pentatonic scale. After mastering these riffs, try transposing them to other keys and positions on the fretboard and also try to create your own Blues riffs using the Minor Pentatonic Scales.

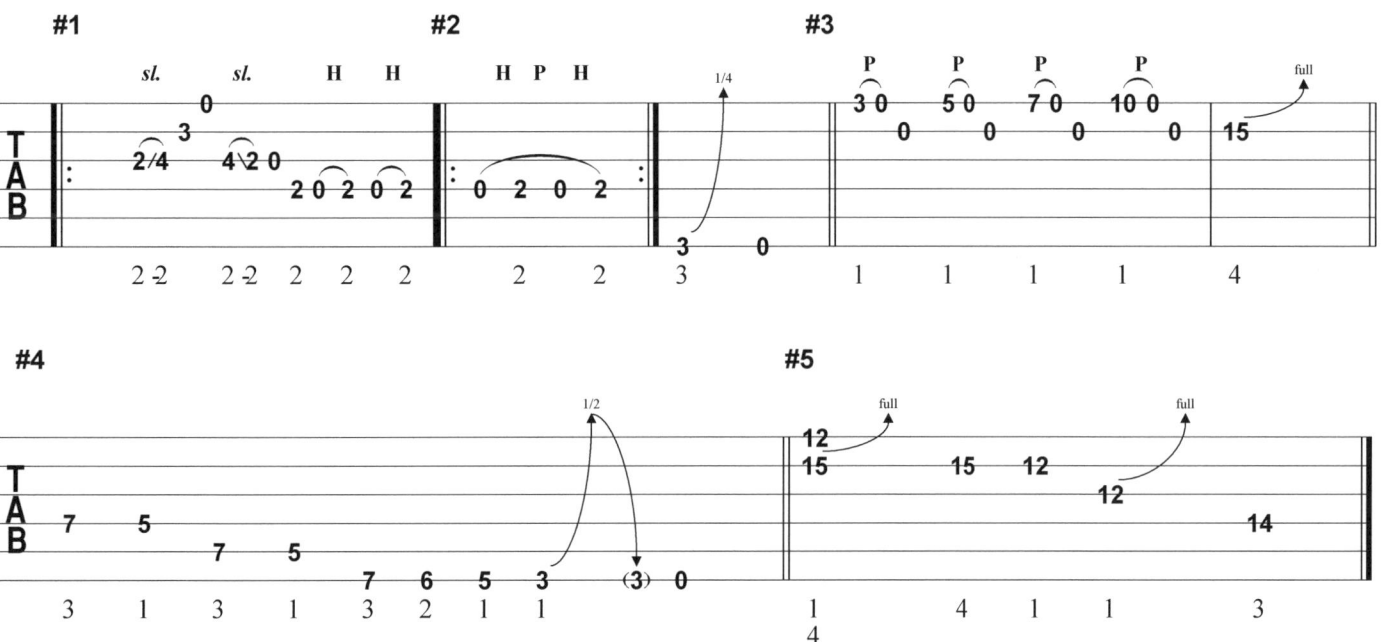

Advanced Jazz/Blues Chords

The following chords are extensions of the regular major and minor chords. The 9th, major 7th and minor 7th chords are commonly used in blues to achieve a jazzier sound. These are all moveable chords and can be transposed to any key.

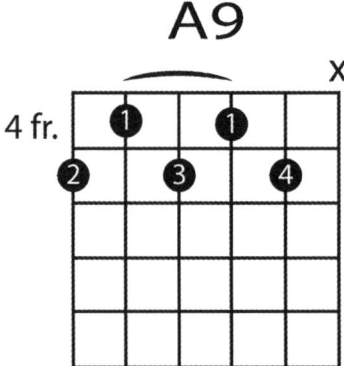
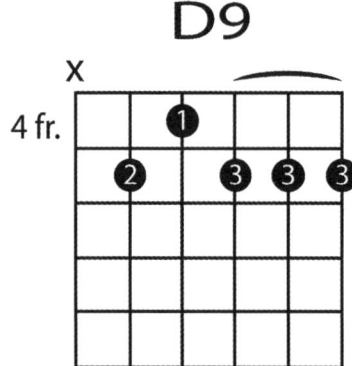
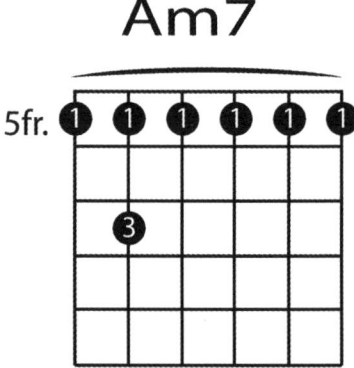
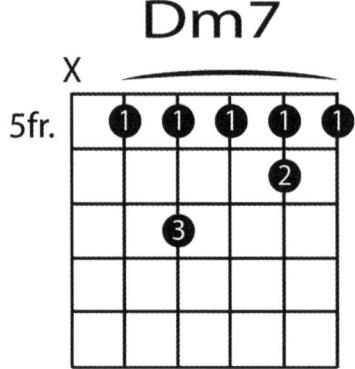
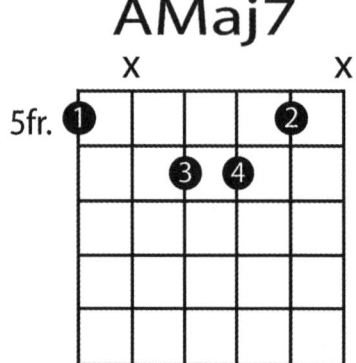
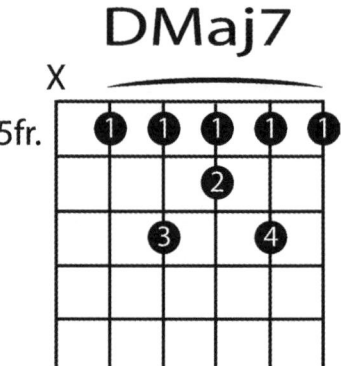

62

The Jazz/Blues Fuze - Complete Rhythm Progression

This jazz blues fuze rhythm is another example of a 12-bar blues progression, the most popular progression used in blues music. This progression uses all 9th chords and is an example of a slow, jazzy blues. The rhythm is played with a straight feel in 6/8 time (six eighth notes per measure). The strumming pattern is indicated below the staff. Count along with the backing track to get the rhythm in your head. The rhythmic feel is in groups of three. Follow the slow blues drum beat and accent your strumming on the downbeats (the first and fourth eighth notes of each measure). When you get the feel down and you're ready to try soloing over the progression, transpose the blues scale positions to the key of A and use them to play leads along with the backing track.

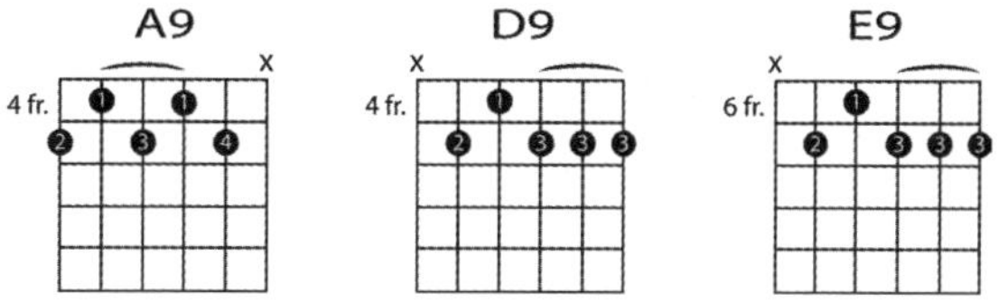

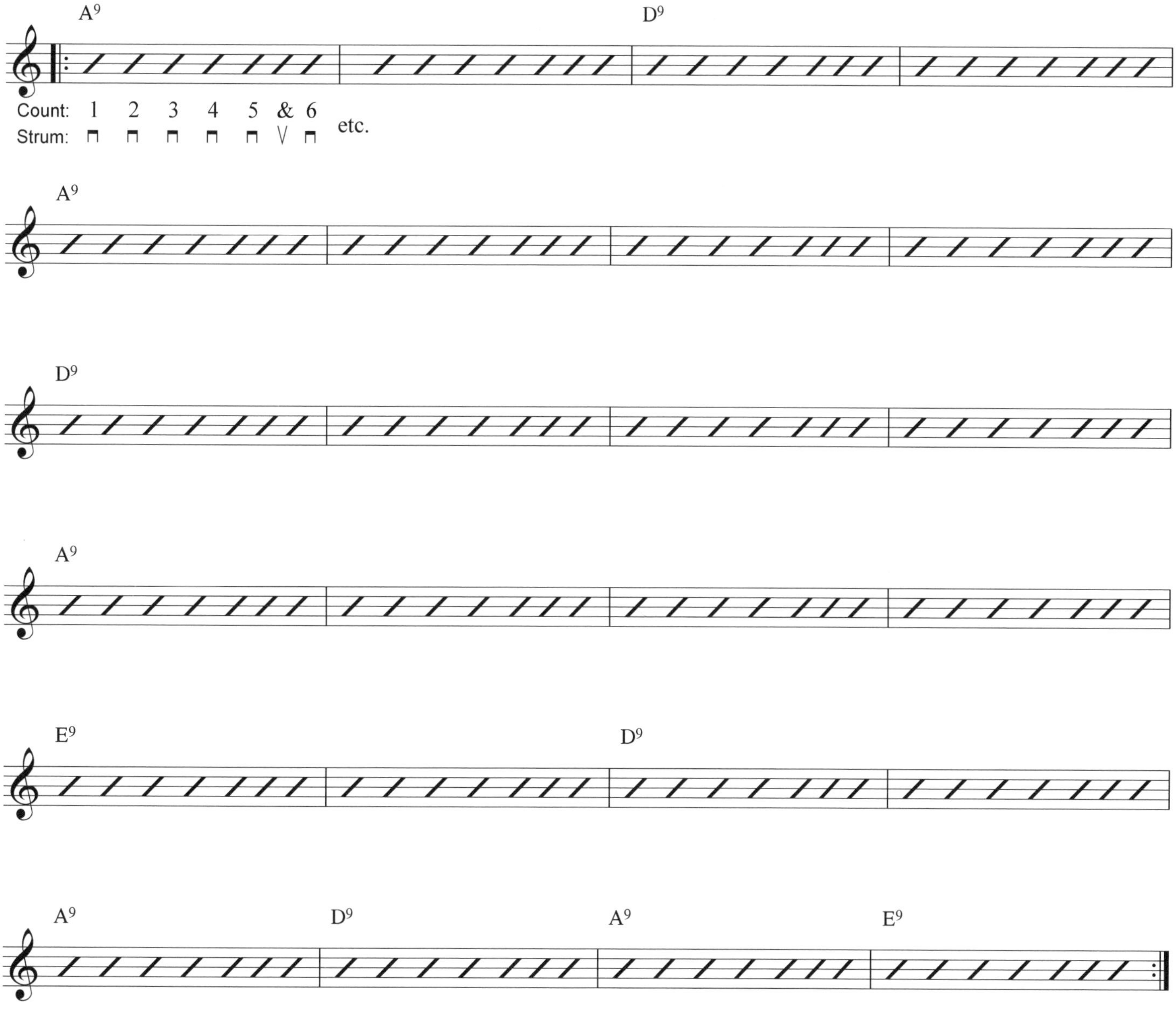

Triplet & Sixteenth Scale Patterns

Let's begin this lesson with a sixteenth lead pattern designed to help build coordination and speed. Use a metronome and increase the tempo gradually over time. The pattern is intended to be played as sixteenth notes, with the bar lines placed after each group of four notes for reading convenience. The example below shows the pattern using a D minor pentatonic scale in the 1st position beginning at the 10th fret, ascending and descending.

Once you get this pattern down. Move onto the second example the triplet lead pattern. Again, go slow and use a metronome to gradually build up your speed. Practicing sequences builds up speed, coordination and finger independence.

Sixteenth Scale Pattern

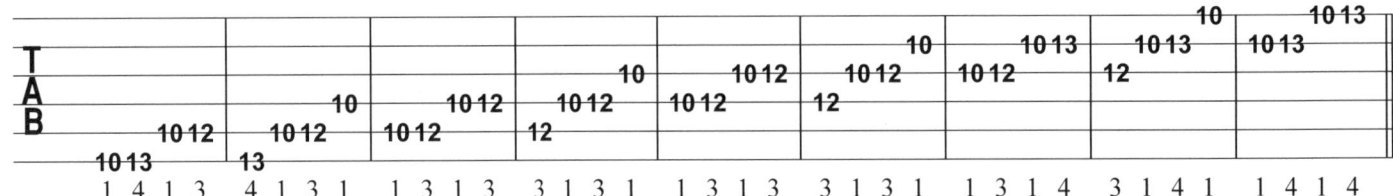

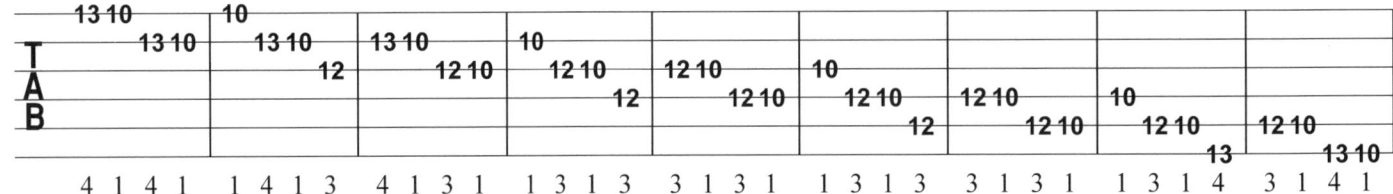

Triplet Scale Pattern

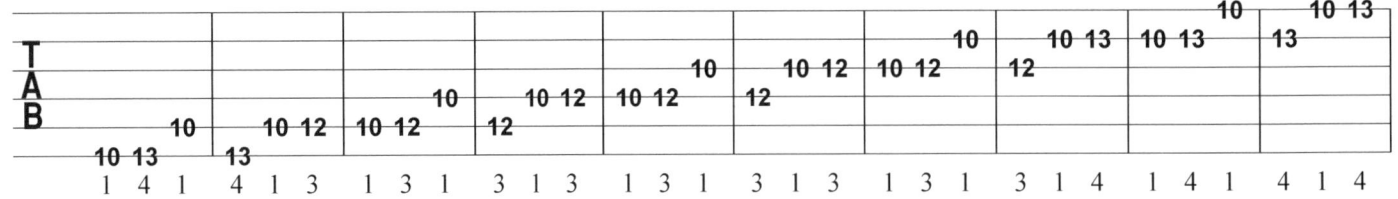

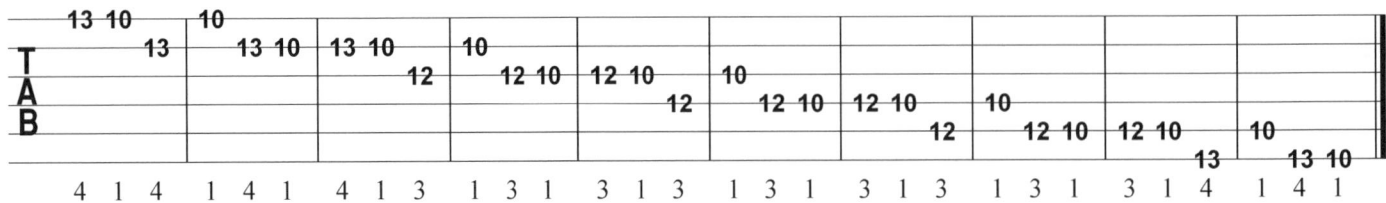

Minor Pentatonic Scale Theory

The way I like to look at this scale is that you isolate a group of notes from the Natural Minor Scale (the full minor scale), this will be discussed later in the course) by taking the 1st, 3rd, 4th, 5th, and 7th notes of the Natural Minor Scale the Minor Pentatonic scale is born. When you play this group of notes you get a unique sound that has that rock/blues feel that makes these scales so popular.

The five Minor Pentatonic Scale positions that you learned in this program are just different places of playing the same five notes on the neck. Unlike other instruments, with guitar you can play the same exact note in more than one place on the neck. The "A" Minor Pentatonic Scale is comprised of these notes A, C, D, E, G and the full Natural Minor scale's notes are as follows A, B, C, D, E, F, G often times players will use a combination of both of these scales while soloing. Make sure you memorize all five positions in all keys so that you can use them to improvise creatively.

Think of these scales as building blocks; sort of like Legos, the second half of the first scale is the first half of the second scale.

Use the scale chart on the the bottom of this page to learn the scales in all keys just pick the letter for the key on the left and follow across to your right to find what fret each position starts on. Remember that 12 frets is one octave, some scale positions will be played in two spots on the neck 12 frets apart.

Minor Pentatonic Key Chart

Key	1st Position	2nd Position	3rd Position	4th Position	5th Position
"A"	5th & 17th	8th	10th	12th & Open	3rd & 15th
"C"	8th	11th	13th & 1st	3rd & 15th	6th & 18th
"E"	12th & Open	3rd & 15th	5th & 17th	7th	10th
"G"	3rd & 15th	6th & 8th	8th	10th	13th & 1st
"B"	7th & 19th	10th	12th	14th & 2nd	5th & 17th
"D"	10th	13th & 1st	3rd & 15th	5th & 17th	8th
"F"	1st & 13th	4th & 16th	6th & 18th	8th	11th

Blues/Rock Rhythm

The following blues rock progression in D is played using a sixteenth note rhythm. The chord changes are based on a I - IV - V progression with the addition of a repeated, single note riff placed between the chords. Use alternate strumming and picking to get the steady, sixteenth notes up to speed. The chords are all barre chords and are shown as full barre chords in the tab staff. You'll notice that these chords are not always fully strummed on the DVD program. This is a good example of interpretation and the use of performance techniques to spice up a simple progression. By varying the accents, muting, or how much of the chord your pick actually strums, you can add character to the sound and style.

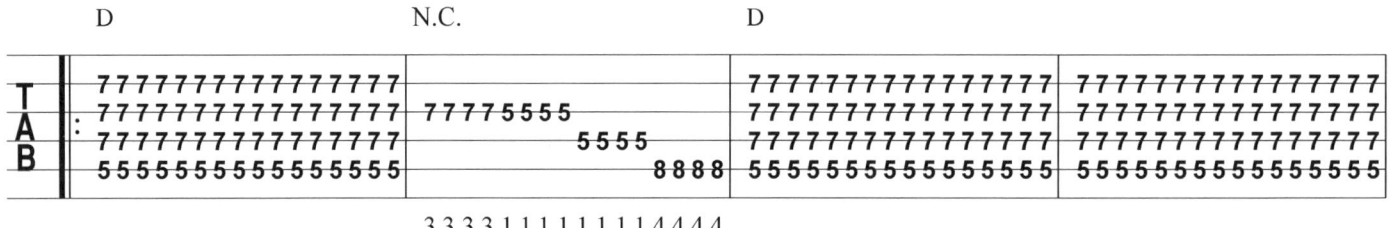

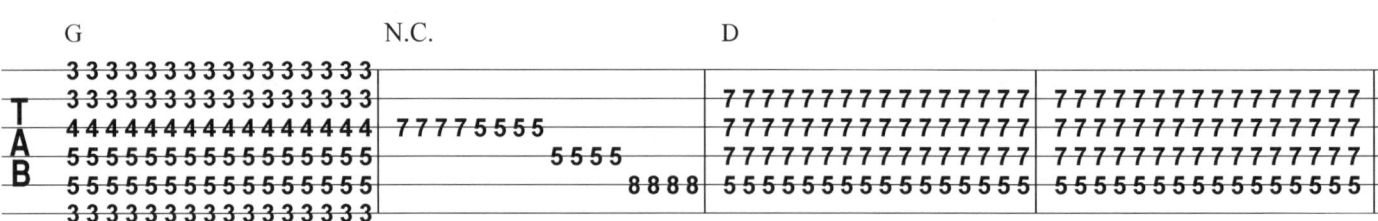

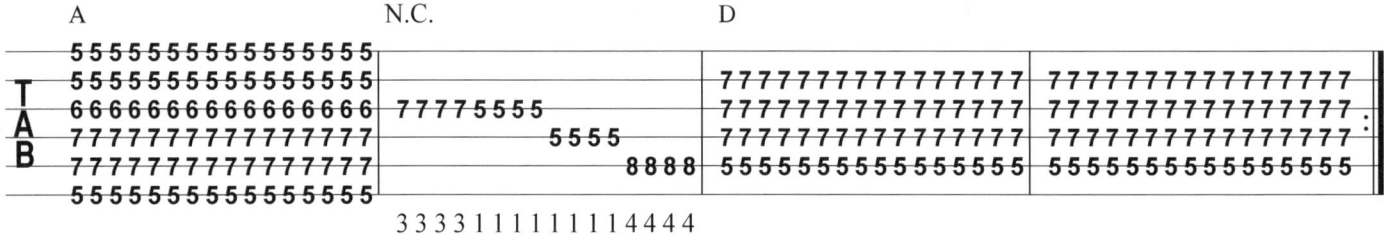

Using the pentatonic scale chart you learned just before this lesson find where all the minor pentatonic scales are in D minor and use them to imrpovise over this progression.

Classic Old School Blues Rhythm & Lead Combo

The turnarounds and endings are underneath the repeat brackets at the end of each repetition. A blues turnaround is a riff at the end of a progression designed to lead smoothly back to the beginning of the rhythm. Blues endings are similar to turnarounds, but are used to conclude songs with a unique flair. Both turnarounds incorporate standard riffs that lead into the V chord (dominant). The final ending uses an open string pull off and hammer on combination riff that leads into the I chord (tonic). The use of dominant seventh chords in the turnarounds and ending give it that classic blues sound.

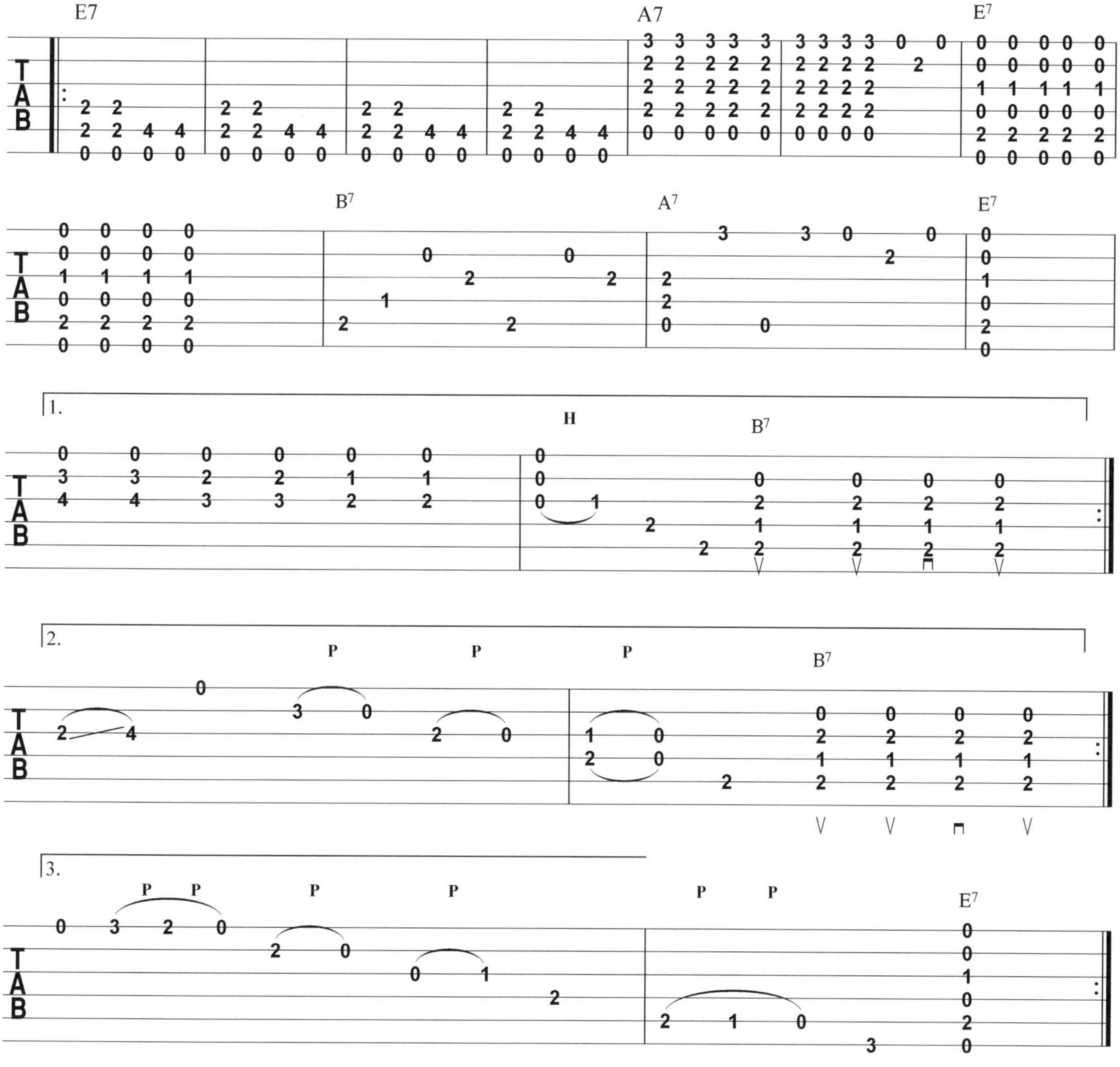

Circle of Fourths Rhythm

The following progression is a slow blues in the key of Am. The rhythm is counted in three's and each chord is arpeggiated (the notes of each chord are picked out separately). Finger and hold the chord in each measure and let its notes ring out together. Play along with the backing track and practice the rhythm's slow ballad feel. The chord change progresses in a pattern of fourths; the distance from one chord to the next is the interval of a fourth. This is a common change that is also used in many musical styles ranging from classical to metal.

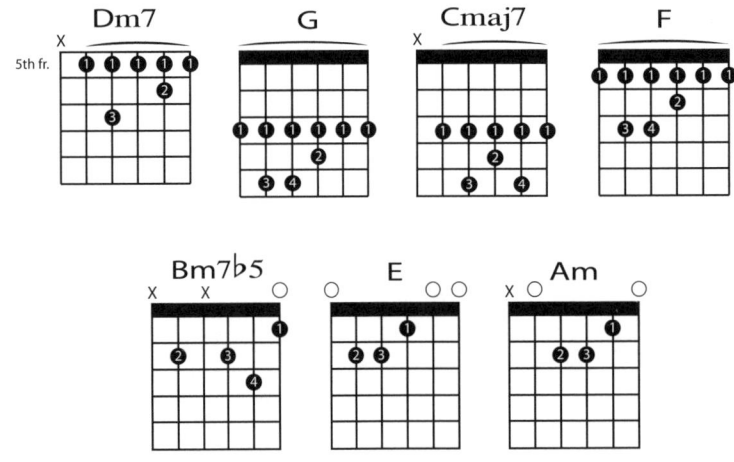

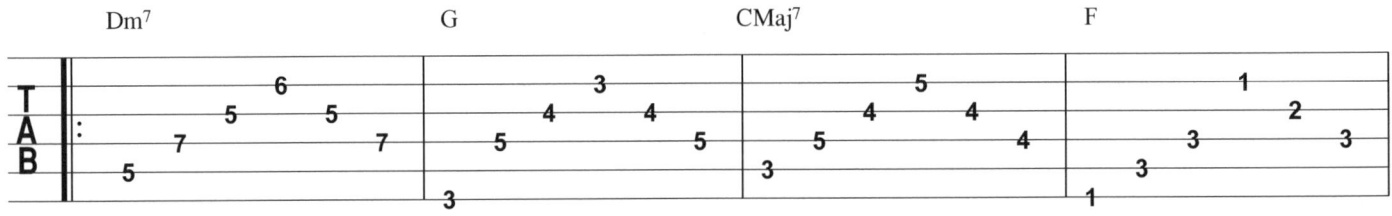

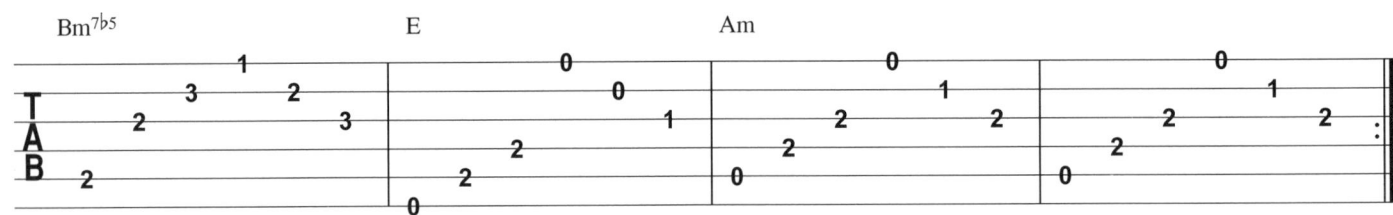

Quick Quote!

"When you strum a guitar you have everything - rhythm, bass, lead and melody."

- David Gilmore / Pink Floyd

Modern Blues Leads
Natural Minor Scales

Many modern Rock and Blues players have incorporated the use of full natural minor scales into their soloing. The pentatonic scales you've already learned are abbreviated versions of the regular major and minor scales. The pentatonic scales contain five notes; the natural minor scale contains seven notes. The word "natural" refers to the fact that the scale is in its original unaltered state. The A natural minor scale is particularly unique because this key contains all natural notes (no sharp or flat notes). The notes in an A natural minor scale are A - B - C - D - E - F - G. The natural minor scale can be used to create more complex and interesting melodies.

1st Position

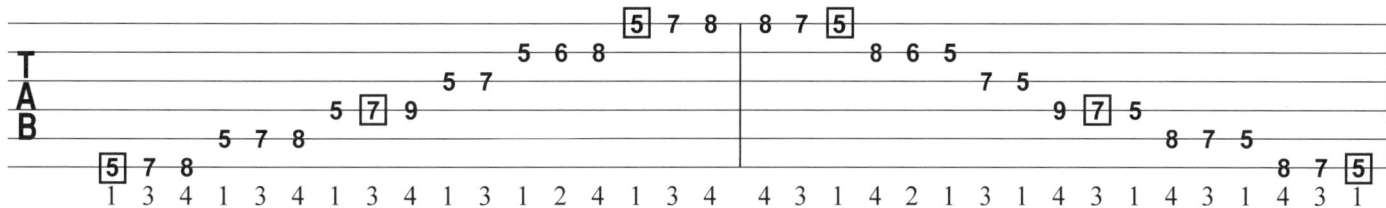

2nd Position

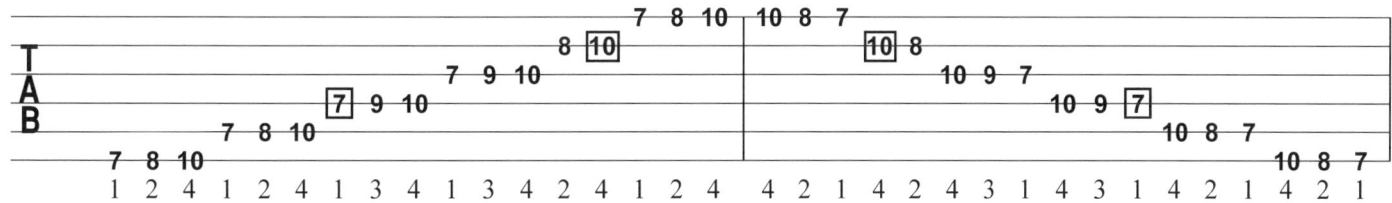

Quick Quote!

"Blues means what milk does to a baby. Blues is what the spirit is to the minister. We sing the blues because our hearts have been hurt, our souls have been disturbed."

- Alberta Hunter

Slide Techniques

Slide guitar is a very popular technique used in blues. A slide is a cylinder worn on the ring finger of your fretting hand that allows you to slide notes and chords in a smooth, steady motion. Slides can be made of glass, metal, brass, or ceramic. You can even spontaneously use a shot glass or beer bottle as a slide.

In order to play pitches in tune with a slide, place the slide directly over the fret bar (not in between the frets). Use the frets as a visual reference point for where the notes will sound in tune. Touch the strings lightly with the slide; don't press down like you're fretting the note. Use the tip of the slide to play single notes or lay it flat to play chords. Open tunings work very well in conjunction with a slide because they allow you to slide full chords with one finger. Guitars that are set up to play with a slide usually have the action (string height) set a little higher than normal to keep the slide from hitting the frets.

A good way to begin to get the slide technique down is to play through the pentatonic scale using a slide. Try it in the 1st position, sliding from the first to the second notes along each string. Remember not to press down with the slide, just allow it to lightly touch the strings.

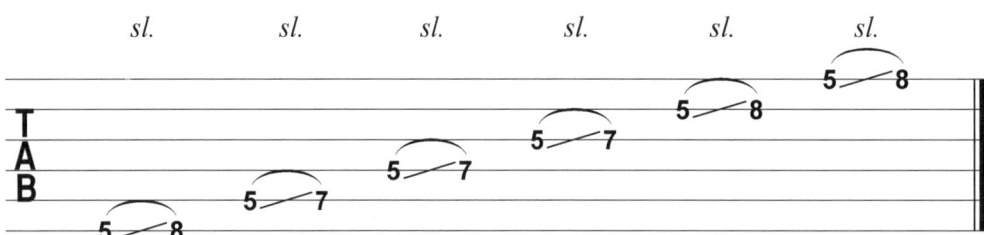

The following exercise is a typical blues rock rhythm played with a slide. This riff has been used to make up countless songs, so it should sound very familiar to you. The first measure (before the repeat sign) is called a pickup. It represents a partial measure of music that leads into the main repeated riff.

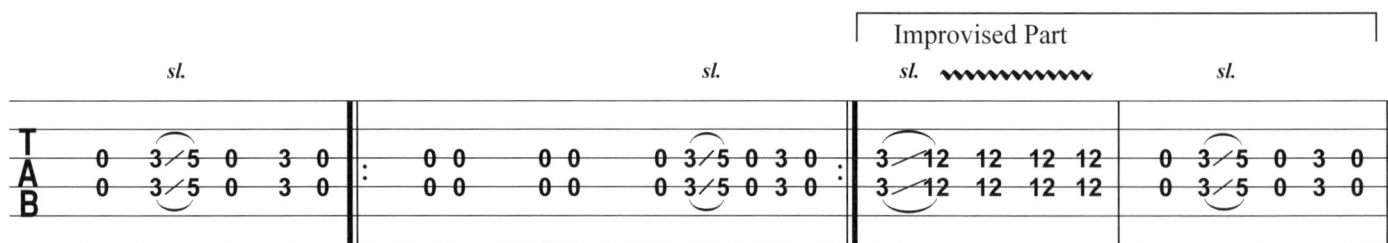

Blues Rhythms

For the last section of this program, let's go over a single note riff rhythm in E. After you learn the rhythm, you can solo over the backing track using the E blues scales and all of the techniques we've covered. The progression is also based on a I - IV - V, 12-bar blues style; the chord names above the tab staff are there as a reference to outline the basic harmony.

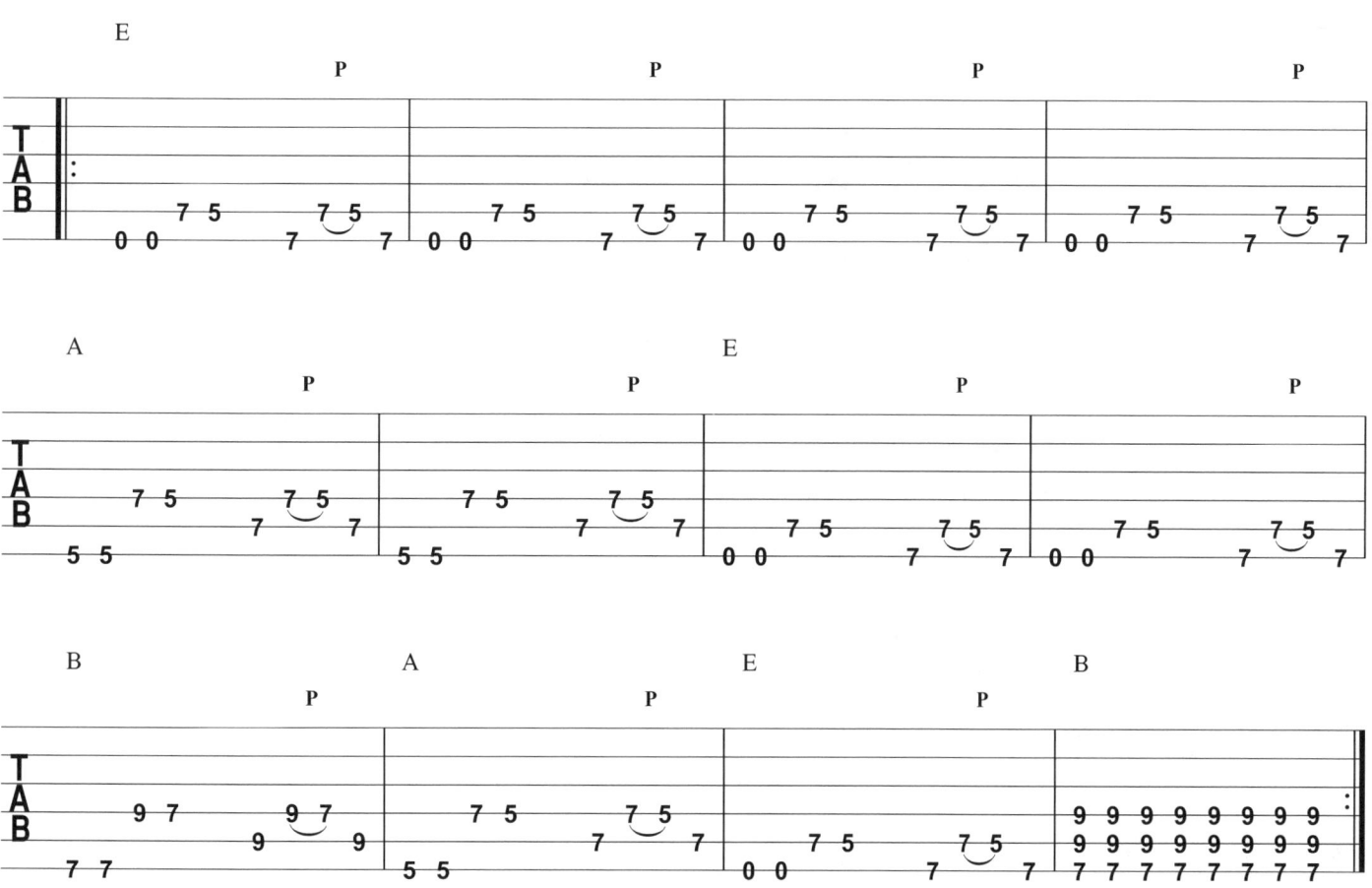

Appendix

Blues Word Search

```
J D N X R O R Y J E J D L N E R J O J U B S L N S N
G U I T A R O C K H O U S E I A S I F L E I J J N L
R F E L I N O U S R H O P T E P D S V B Y N O S J E
S Y C A T M D I U L N O A B J S R E T A W Y D D U M
L G R O U S N R I A L L E A D B E L L Y J J V S K I
N N O S N H O J T R E B O R N O T P A L C C I R E A
J I S L S U S N N E R F L O W N I L W O H B H J J
A K S L I T R U H N H O J I P P I S S I S S I M O A
O E R A L B E R T C O L L I N S W L R O B I N N I N
N I O Y L L F V B S O I L D N Y Y O L J B S I E N I
I D A A J C F I I M K D B B K I N G G I B A B B T S
O D D M S I E E G E E E A H J J N R G S E L I D S J
A E S N S E J D B U R D V E O I H J S J U D J I O O
S R U H U N N L I A D A E R F L O R R E B C I X N P
G F N O T R O M L L O R Y L L E J L S O H H I X H L
O M I J A I M B L I S J O V T O L S I I L R J H O I
I O A O L O E L B I A A N U A A H M C U D Y D T U N
A N U E S R L U R I S E R Y T U B A O N I A N I S S
J E H E T X D T O T G N T E F K G L E R R G U M E D
S O R K U D N T O L E Y R F I O T H U S E L O S R L
L C I E Y U I A N R E S L S B F I U A E N J R E Y M
S N L G N S L T Z O R E O L L M I G I N S W A I H F
G O U I R N B L Y E D M U P I G Y L E T N O N M U O
E Y R U L A R M U R U E B J C B B N P R L R R A E E
U I S F I R K D D I S T O R T I O N R M S O U M O S
C H O L O E E N O R D N E R E R O N T J A S T E C F
```

Find the 38 words below in the puzzel above. The words go in all directions; forwards, backwords and diagnally. Answer key is on page 80.

Albert Collins
Albert King
Amplifier
BB King
Big Bill Broonzy
Big Joe Turner
Billy Gibbons
Blind Lemon Jefferson
Blues Shuffle
Buddy Guy
Chicago Blues
Crossroads
Delta Blues

Distortion
Elmore James
Eric Clapton
Freddie King
Guitar
Howlin Wolf
Janis Joplin
Jelly Roll Morton
Jimi Hendrix
John Lee Hooker
John Mayall
Johnny Winter
Juke Joints

Lead Belly
Mamie Smith
Mississippi John Hurt
Muddy Waters
Otis Rush
Robert Johnson
Rock House
Slide
Son House
Stevie Ray Vaughan
Turnaround
Willie Dixon

Changing Your Strings

Old guitar strings may break or lose their tone and become harder to keep in tune. You might feel comfortable at first having a teacher or someone at a music store change your strings for you, but eventually you will need to know how to do it yourself. Changing the strings on a guitar is not as difficult as it may seem and the best way to learn how to do this is by practicing. Guitar strings are fairly inexpensive and you may have to go through a few to get it right the first time you try to restring your guitar. How often you change your strings depends entirely on how much you play your guitar, but if the same strings have been on it for months, it's probably time for a new set.

Most strings attach at the headstock in the same way, however electric and acoustic guitars vary in the way in which the string is attached at the bridge. Before removing the old string from the guitar, examine the way it is attached to the guitar and try to duplicate that with the new string. Acoustic guitars may use removeable bridge pins that fasten the end of the string to the guitar by pushing it into the bridge and securing it there. On some electric guitars, the string may need to be threaded through a hole in the back of the body

Follow the series of photos below for a basic description of how to change a string. Before trying it yourself, read through the quick tips for beginners on the following page.

Use a string winder to loosen the string.

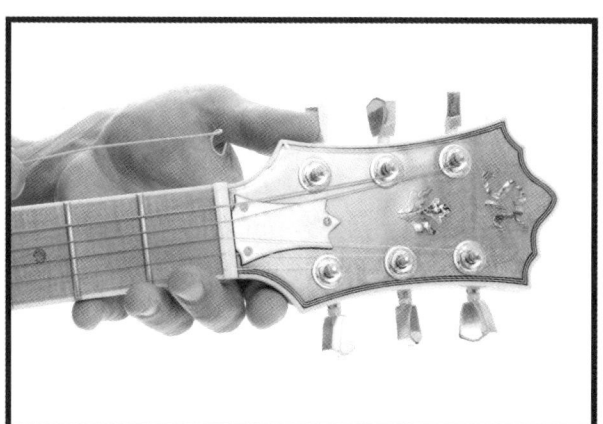
Remove the old string from the post.

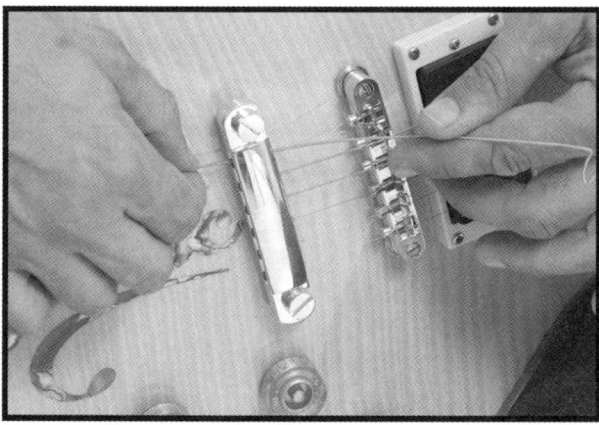
Pull the string through the bridge and discard it.

Remove the new string from the packaging and uncoil it.

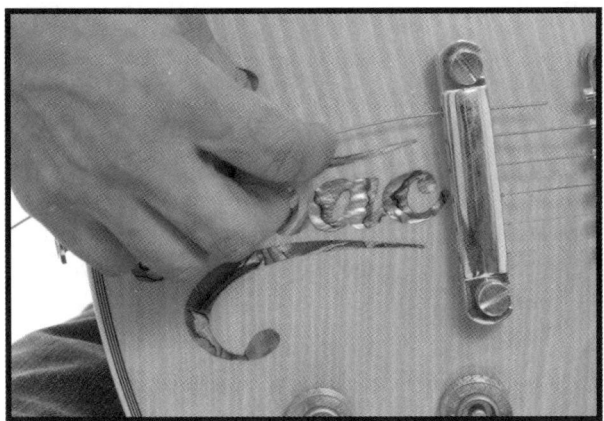
Thread the end of the new string through the bridge.

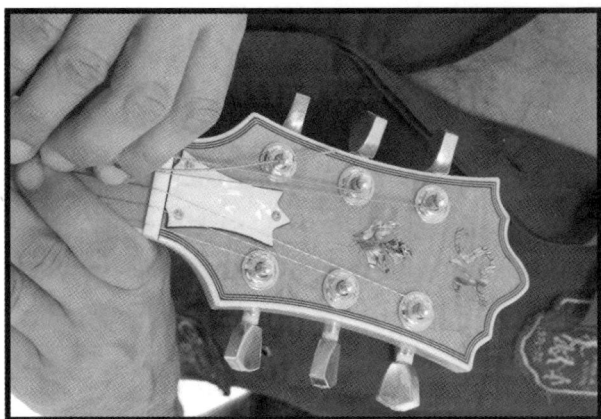
Pull the string along the neck and thread it through the small hole on the tuning post.

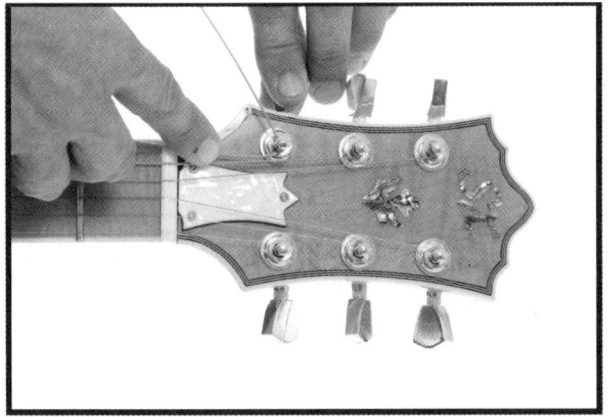
Hold the string in place just after the nut with your finger and tighten up the slack in the string with tthe maching head.

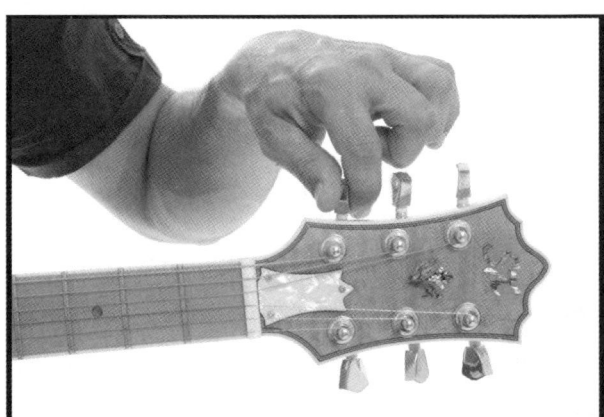
Carefully tighten the string and tune it to the proper pitch.

You can cut the old string off the guitar but you may want to unwind it instead and save it as a spare in case you break a string later.

Check to make sure you have the correct string in your hand before putting it on the guitar. The strings may be color coded at the end to help you identify them.

Be sure to wind the string around the tuning post in the proper direction (see photos), and leave enough slack to wind the string around the post several times. The string should wind around the post underneath itself to form a nice, neat coil.

Once the extra slack is taken up and the string is taught, tune it very gradually to pitch, being careful not to overtighten and accidentally break the new string.

Once the string is on the guitar and tightened up, you can cut the excess string sticking out from the tuning post with a wire cutter. The sharp tail end that is left can be bent downward with the wire cutter to get it out of the way and avoid cutting or stabbing your finger on it.

Check the ends of the string to make sure it is sitting correctly on the proper saddle and space on the nut.

New strings will go out of tune very quickly until they are broken in. You can gently massage the new string with your thumbs and fingers once it's on the guitar, slightly stretching the string out and helping to break it in. Then retune the string and repeat this process a few times for each string.

Practice Tips

To ensure constant progress and high motivation you have to develop practice habits that will keep you interested and challenged. Great practice habits will result in better overall playing and take you to the next level. As you move forward with your practice routine there are a few things you should do:

1. Practice consistently, I have had many students come to me and say I missed four days of practice and on the fifth day I played 4 hours. This is not the way to practice and see results because you do not give your fingers a chance to gain muscle memory. Practice every day even if it is for a short amount of time, be consistent.

2. Have a practice spot set up so you can have privacy to focus on your playing. It is a great idea to have a music stand to help position your music so you can sit comfortably. I remember when I started playing and I would lay my music on my bed and twist my neck to try to read and hold my guitar up properly, it was a real pain in the neck!

3. Always have your guitar out of the case, I use the expression "out of sight out of mind" if you see your guitar sitting there on a stand you are more prone to pick it up and play. When it's in a case under your bed its work to take it out and this may detour you from practicing. Besides when your friends come over your house and see your guitar they will be impressed!

4. Set a scheduled practice time each day, say you want to practice before school or work every day make this time a routine then later in the day you can play for fun and jam a little more.

Creating a Practice Routine

As you evolve as a guitarist you will be constantly changing your practice outline. You should combine a series of components in your practice routine that will help you develop all aspects of your playing. Here is a list of my favorites.

1. Technique exercises for the left hand –
This is an exercise that challenges the coordination of your fretting hand. Many hammer on and pull off exercises work well to develop your fretting hand. These are usually repetitive exercises. Build speed gradually and practice them with a metronome

2. Technique exercises for developing your picking -
This is an exercise that challenges the coordination of your pick hand. Multiple string repetitive sequences are great pick exercises. You should build speed gradually and practice these with a metronome

3. Scales and patterns –
Use seven note and pentatonic scales in all different keys. Practice them with patterns of 2's, 3's and 4's always using alternate picking. Mix it up week by week to challenge your fingers.

4. Performance pieces –
This would be a song that you wish to learn that you haven't started yet. Pick a song that you want to learn have it on CD or tab and start picking it apart…literally!

5. Creating leads over progressions (backing tracks) -
This is where you get creative and jam a little to make melodies and leads. You can use jam backing tracks that have progressions of bass, drums and rhythm. Another way to do this is to pick your favorite CD and jam along pretending that you are a member of the band. Mimic the lead singer's melodies and play riffs and phrasings along with the track. This is a great way to learn to play melodically.

6. Classical pieces –
I like to use single string classical pieces here like Mozart Sonata #11 or #16 , they are almost always very challenging and they sound cool with a bit of distortion kicked in too.

7. Fun playing –
This is where you play things you know already, crank the amp up and rip into some guitar and have some fun!

8. Mental perception (visualization away from your instrument) –
Even though you may not be able to have your guitar with you all day long every day that doesn't mean you can't practice. Visualization is so important. Just going through your scales and the notes on the neck in your mind paints a visual picture that will help you to fly across the strings with ease. When you can see it in your mind your fingers will follow.

Practice Log

Here is a chart you can copy to keep track of your practice routine as well as your progress. The example line shows that all week you practice the E blues scales and log your final metronome speed.

Task	Day 1	Day 2	Day 3	Day 4	Day 5	Day 6	Day 7
E Blues Scales w/ Metronome	✓ 60BPM	✓ 60BPM	✓ 65BPM	✓ 70BPM	✓ 85BPM	✓ 90BPM	✓ 95BPM

Minor Pentatonic Scales

A Minor

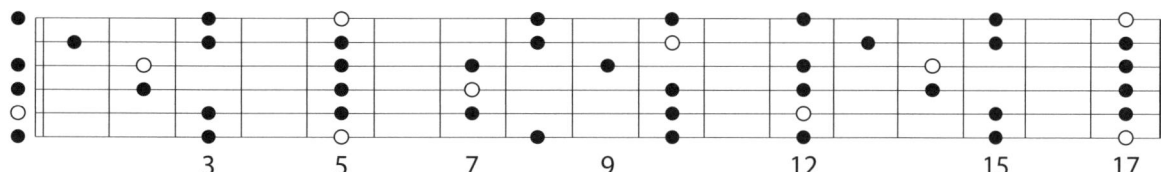

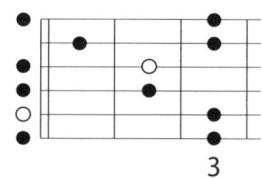 4th Position

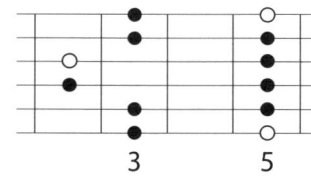 5th Position

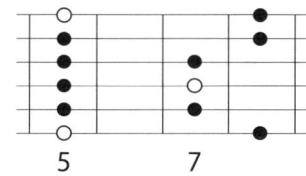 1st Position

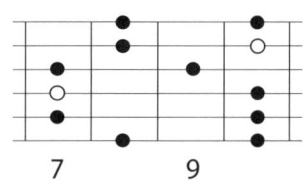 2nd Position

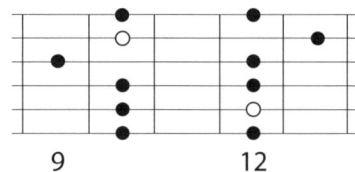 3rd Position

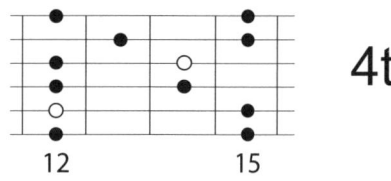 4th Position

Major Pentatonic Scales

A Major

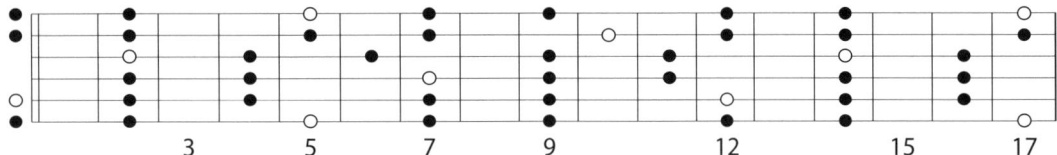

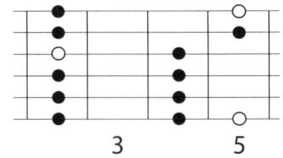 5th Position

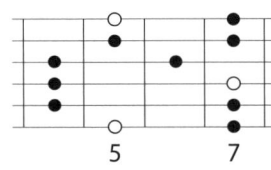 1st Position

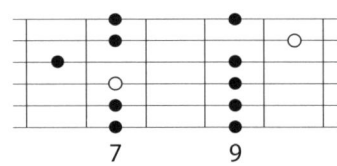 2nd Position

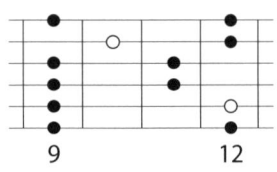 3rd Position

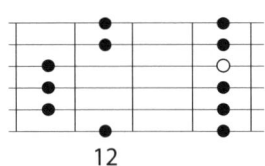 4th Position

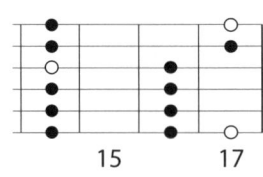 5th Position

Blues Scales

A Blues

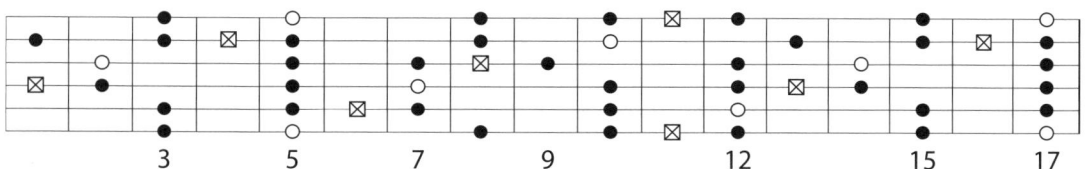

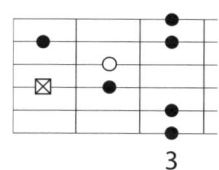 4th Position

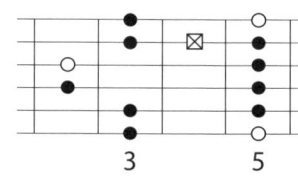 5th Position

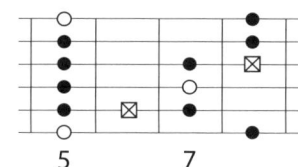 1st Position

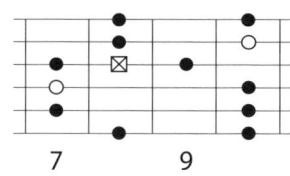 2nd Position

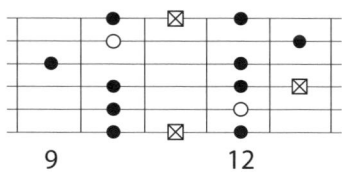 3rd Position

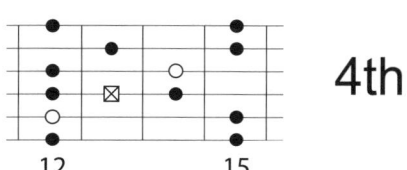 4th Position

Common Blues Progression Variations

The following examples are typical variations of the Blues progression. There are many variations that have been used throughout the decades. All of the following progressions are written in the key of "C." Transpose these progressions to all of the keys. Below each measure you will see the chord/key function to help you transpose these progressions easier. If you are unfamiliar with some of these chords, make sure you get a copy of "The Only Chord Book You Wil Ever Need" from Rock House.

Double "V" Turnaround 12 Bar

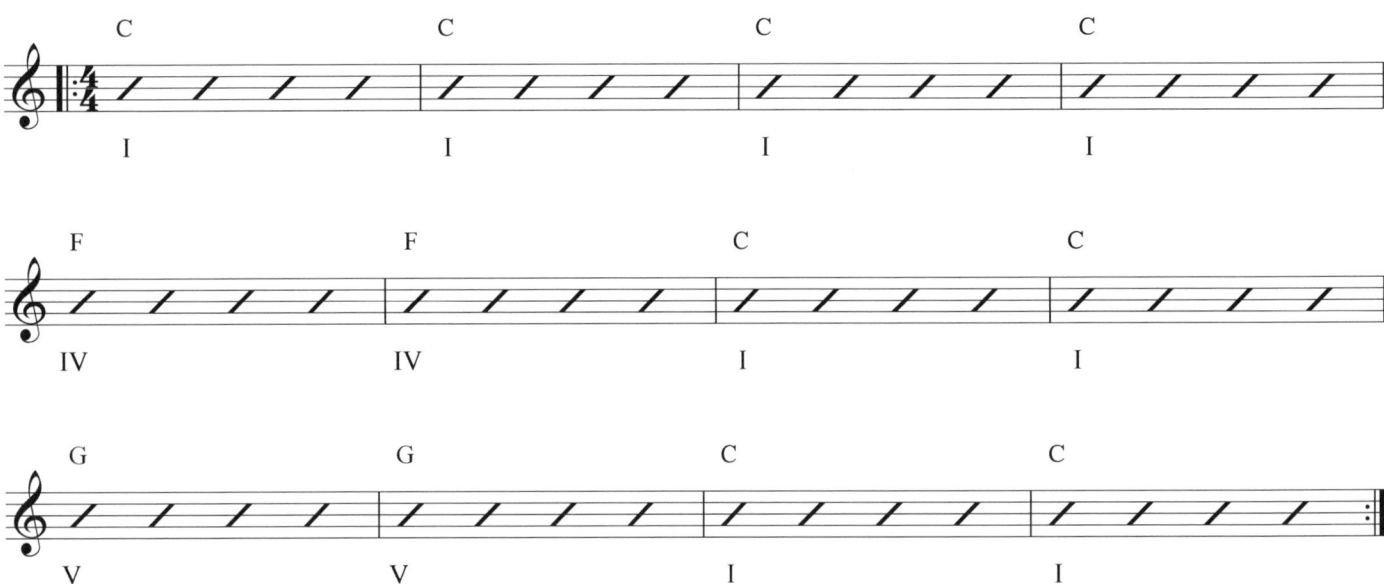

Substituting THE "iv" Chord with a "I" Minor Chord

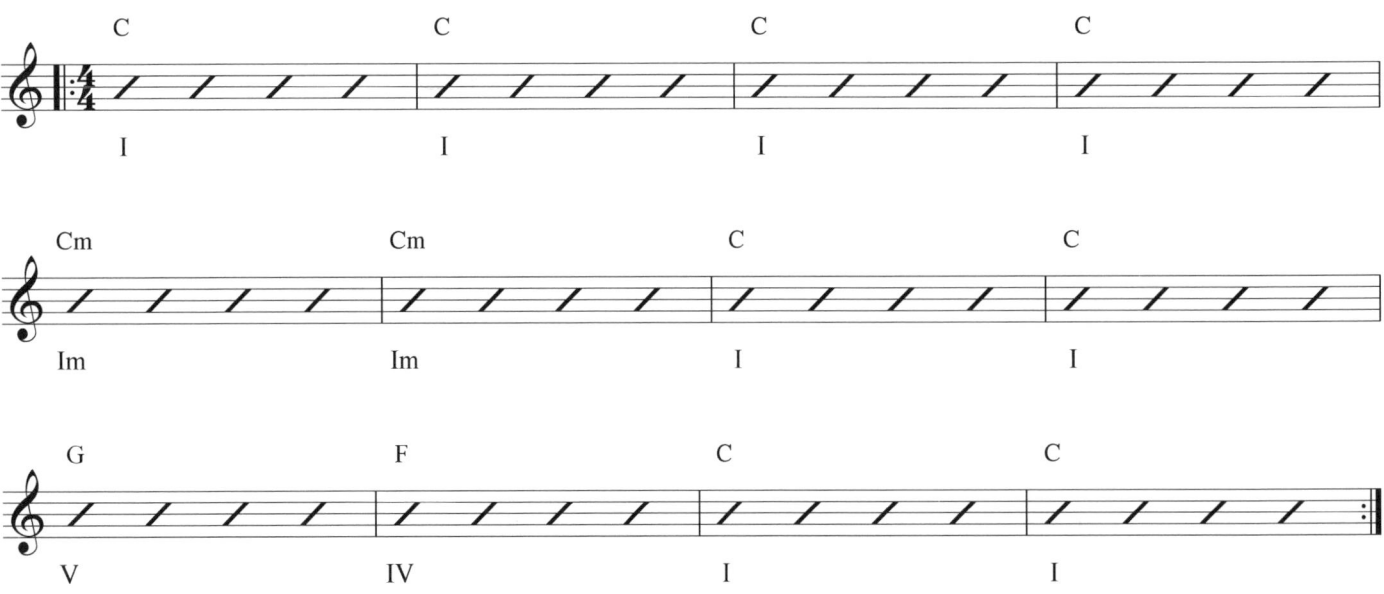

Using a Dominant Chord Before Chord Changes

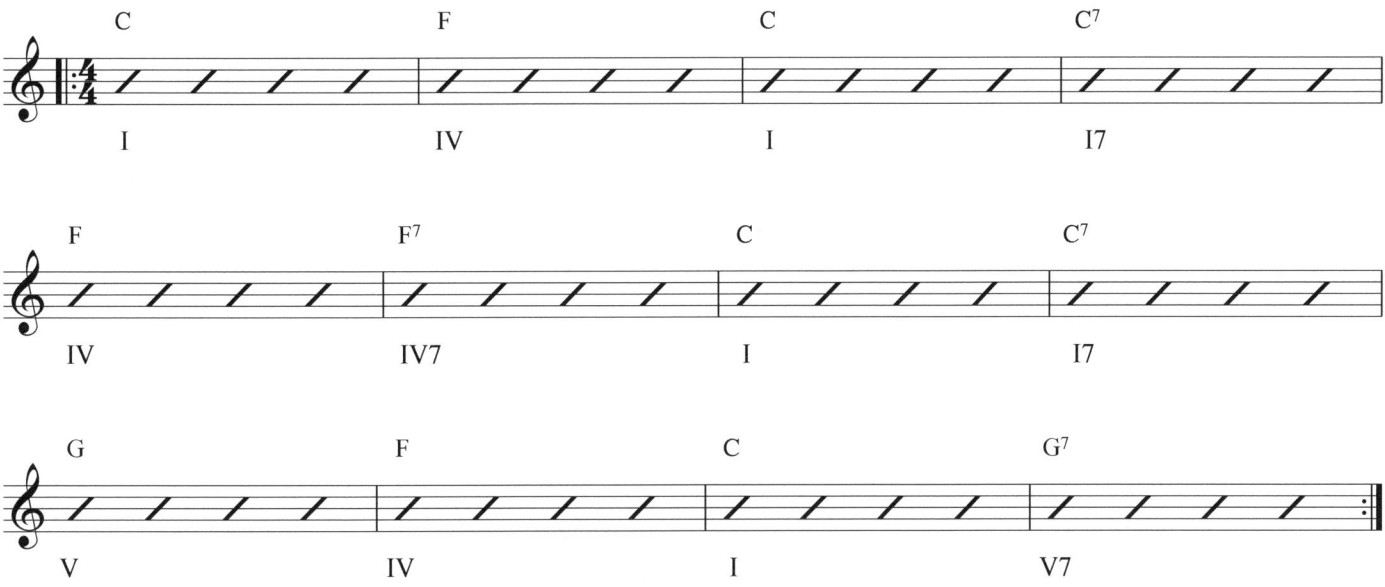

12 Bar Basie Blues Chord Progression

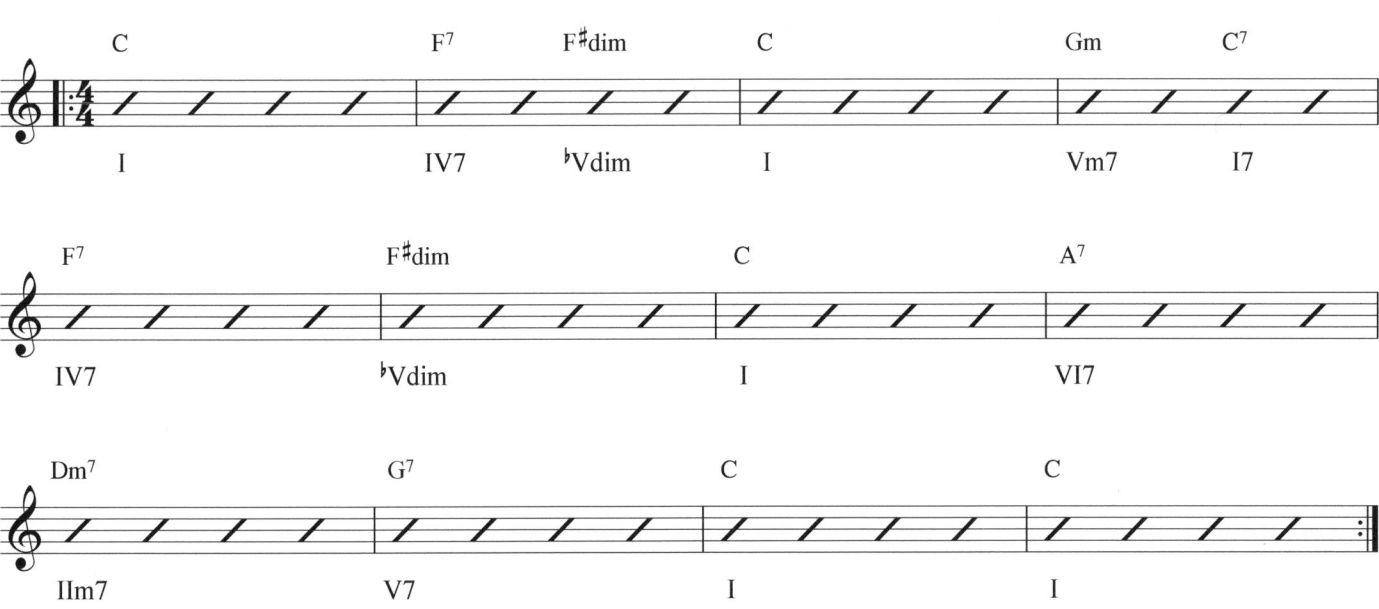

Basic Jazz/Blues Progression

Notice the close similarities to the 12 Bar Basie Blues Progression you just learned.

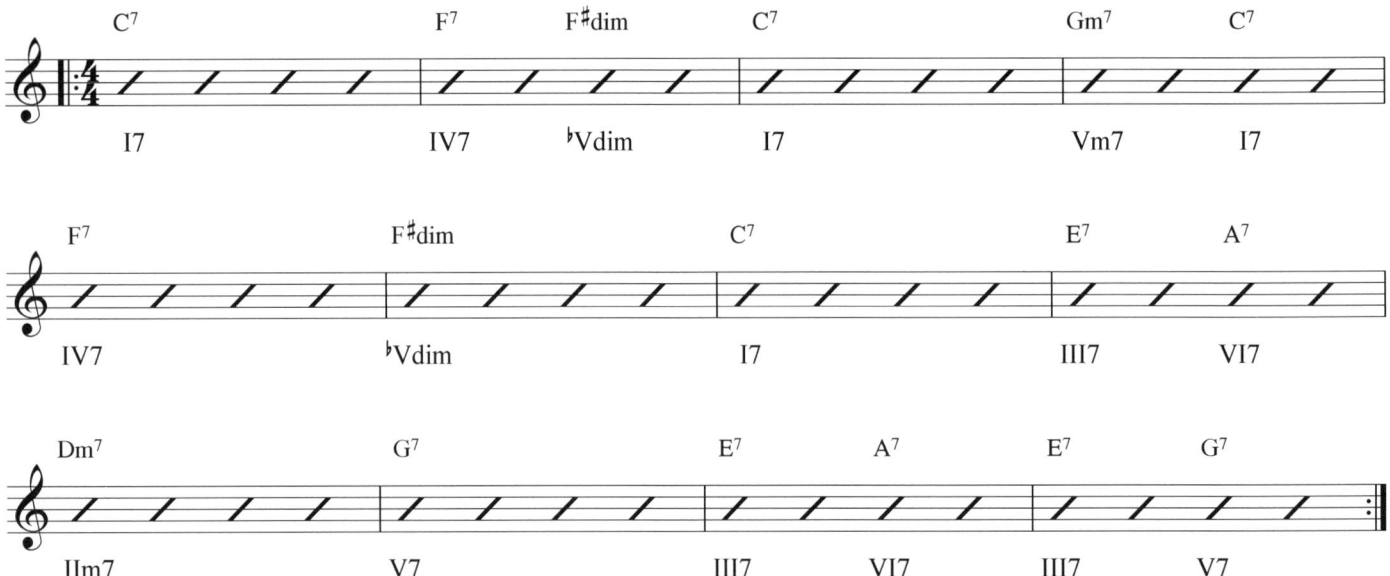

12 Bar Minor Blues Progression

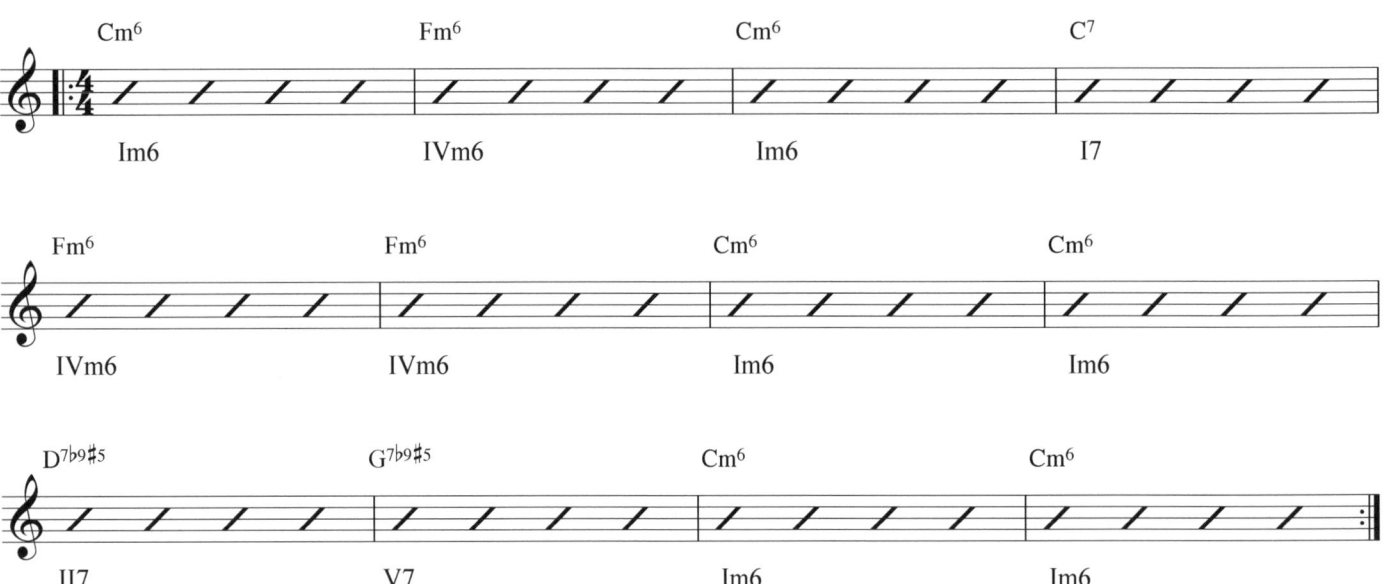

Some Blues progressions are more or less than 12 bars long. Here are a few examples of some different blues forms you may encounter on your journey to being a great Blues musician.

8 Bar Blues Progression

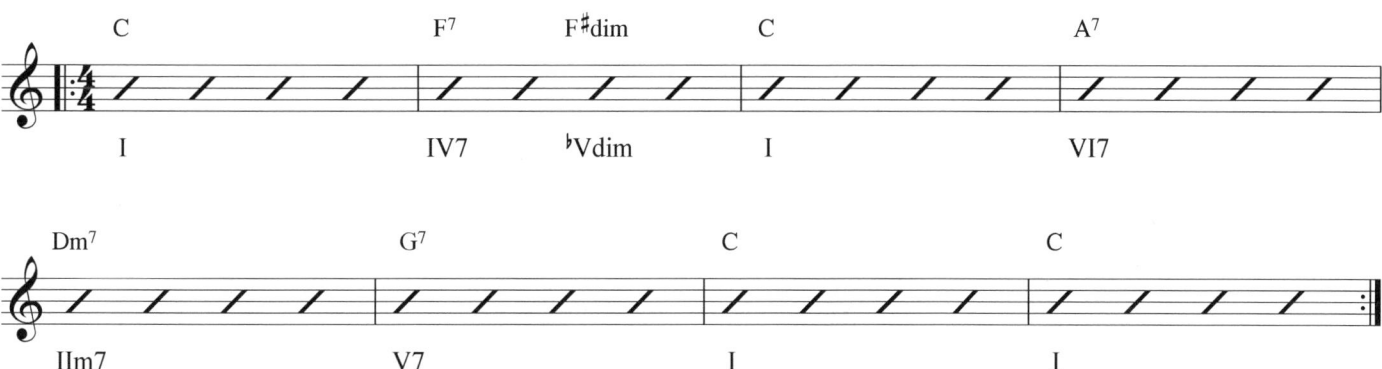

16 Bar Blues Progression

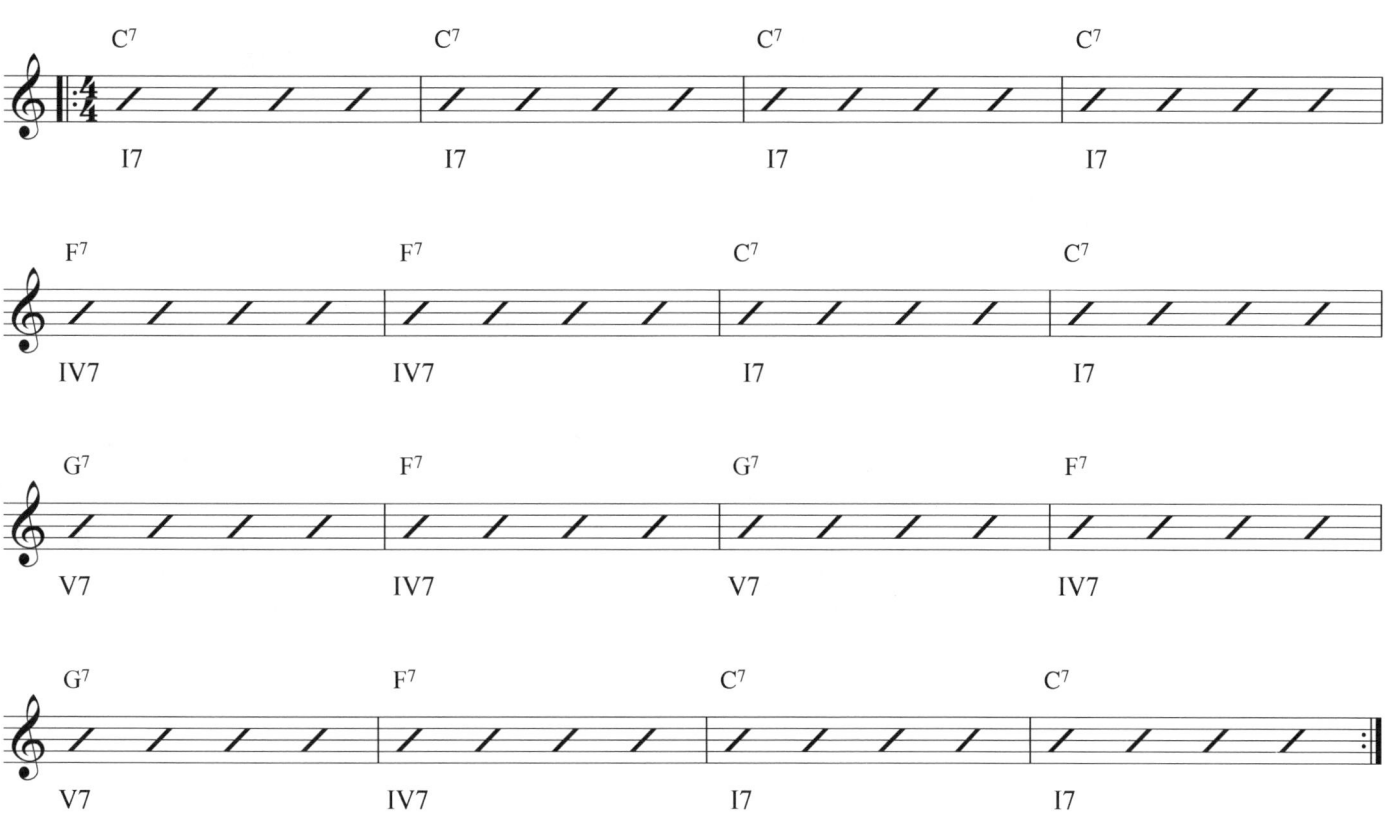

Blues Chord Glossary

Chords are the building blocks for songs. By learning new chords you expand your horizons for building song structures. You need to have chord knowledge to create your own masterpiece. I've compiled a group of chords that are great for blues music. They are all root C chords but many are movable and can be played in any key by moving them up or down the neck.

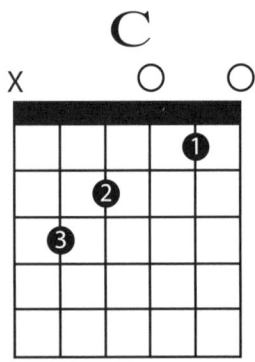

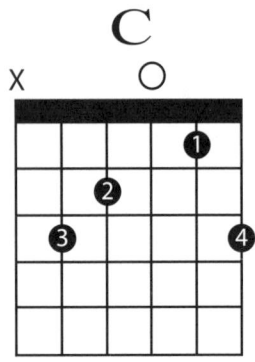
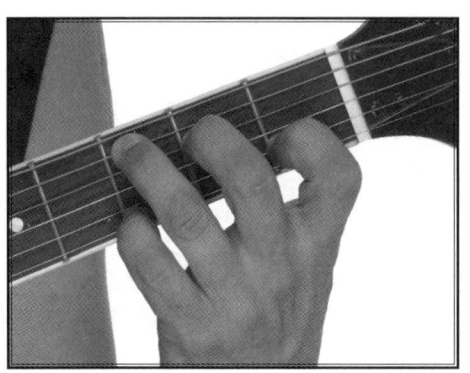

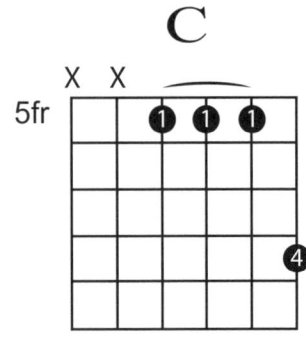

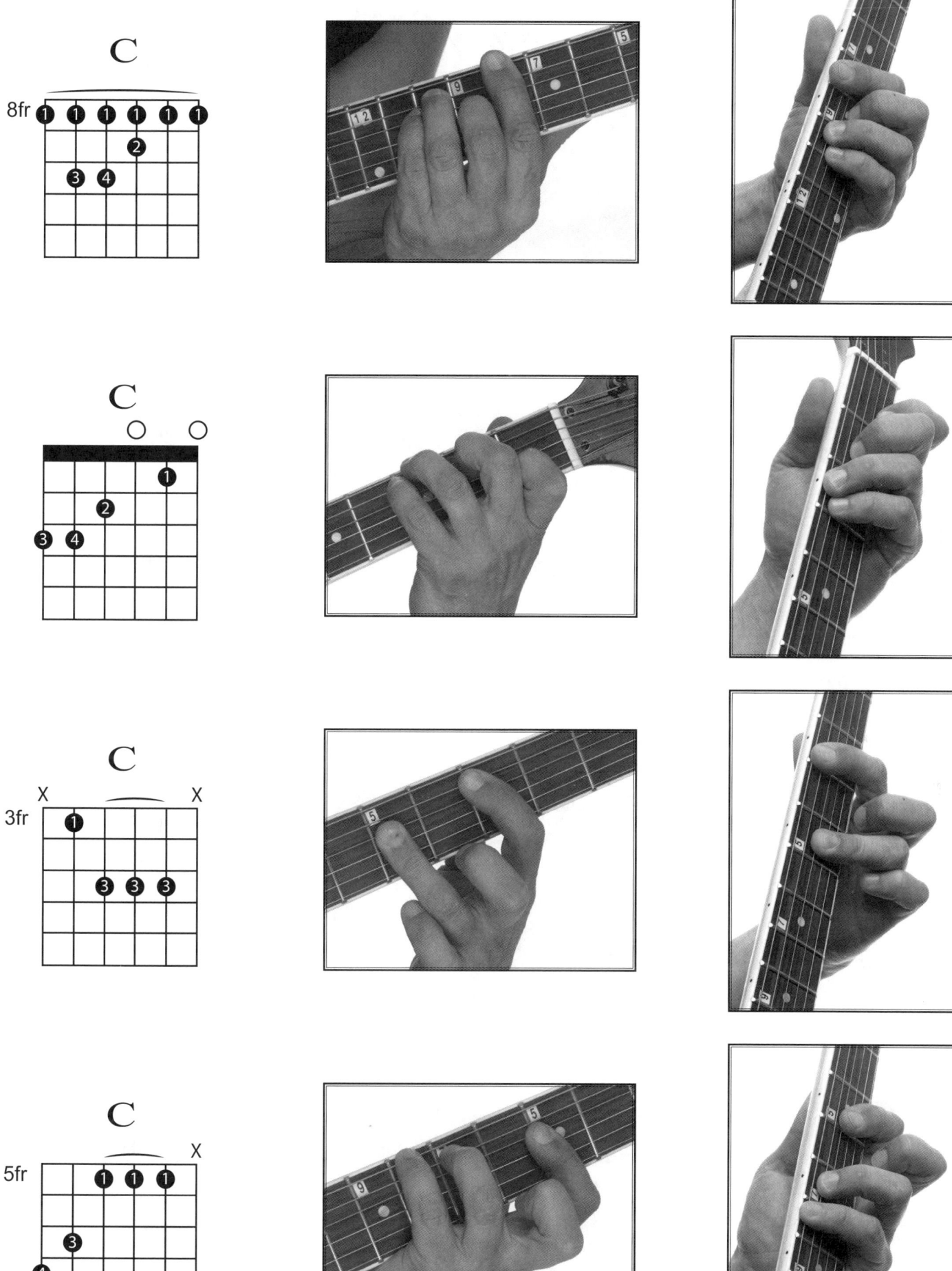

C

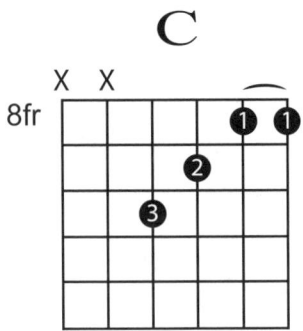  

Csus⁴

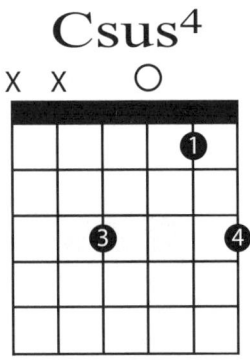  

Csus⁴

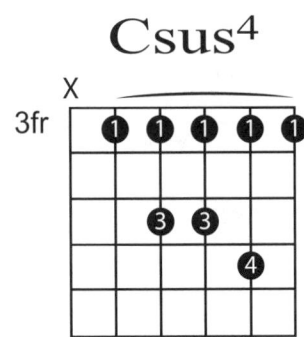  

Csus⁴

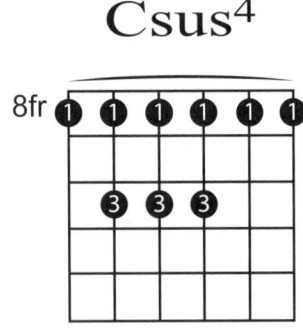  

Csus²

3fr

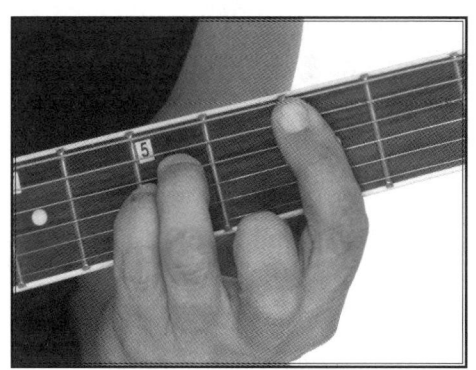

Csus²

5fr

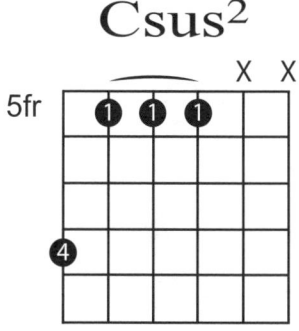

Csus²

10fr

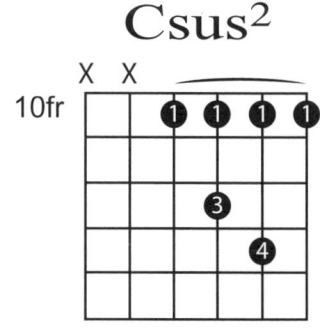

C⁶

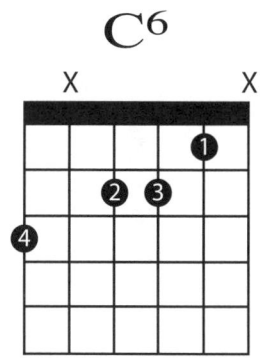

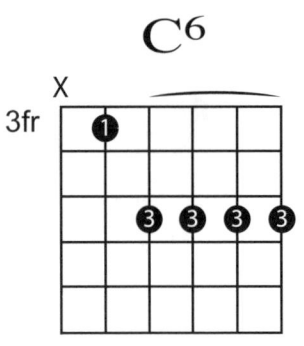

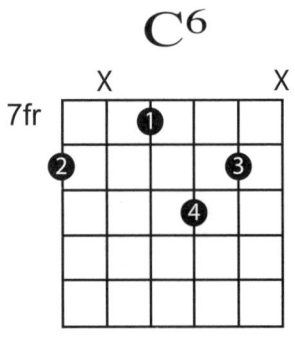

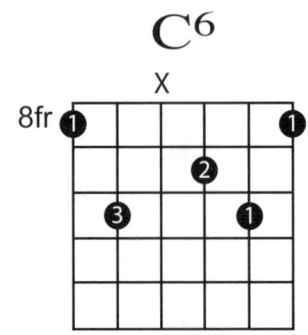

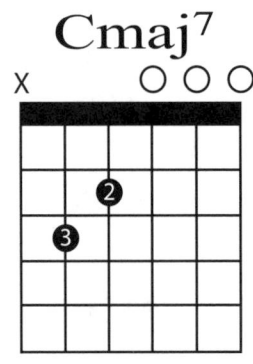
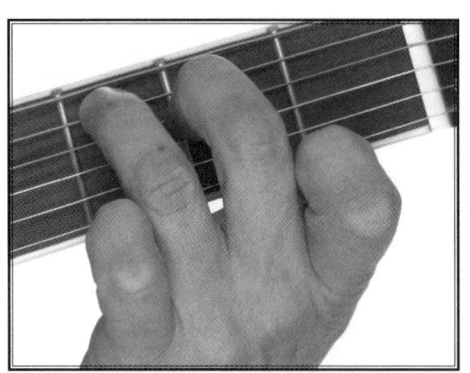

Cmaj7

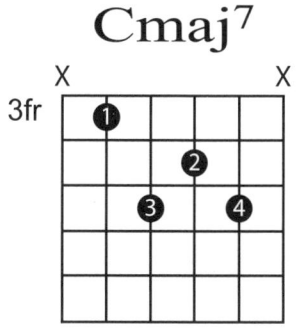

Cmaj7

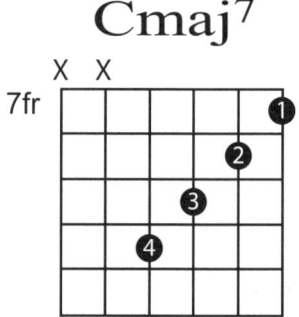

Cmaj7

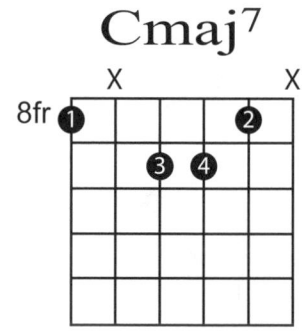
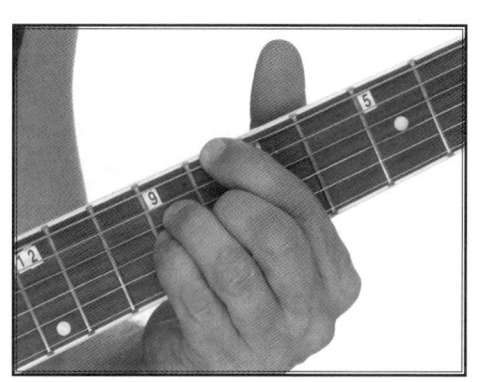

Cmaj9

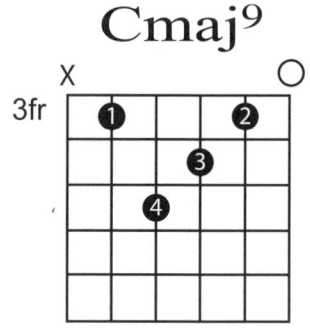

Cmaj⁹

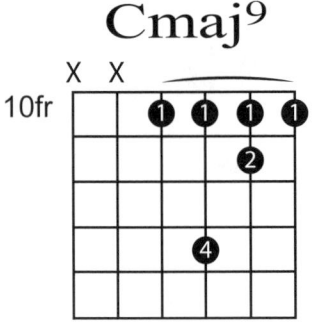 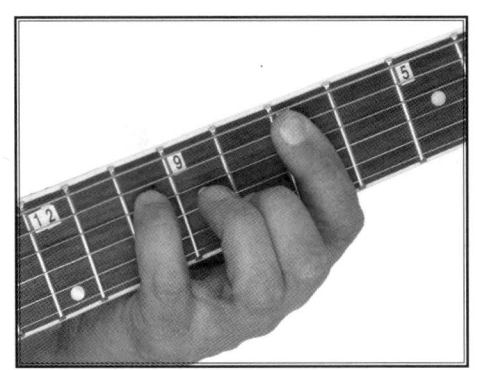 

Cmaj¹³

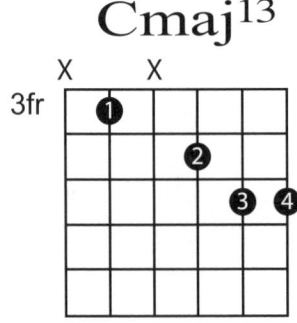  

Cmaj¹³

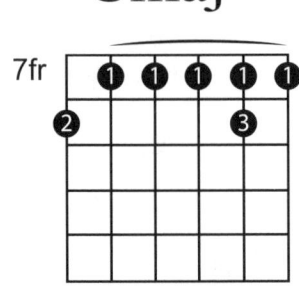  

Cm

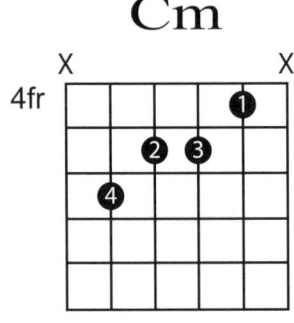  

Cm

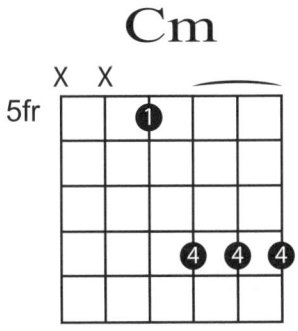
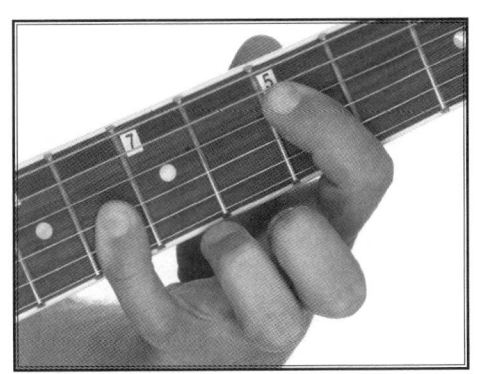

Cm

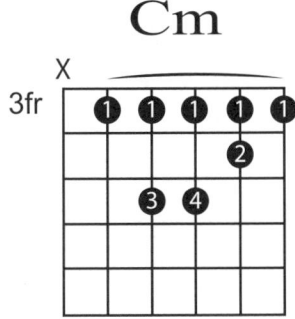
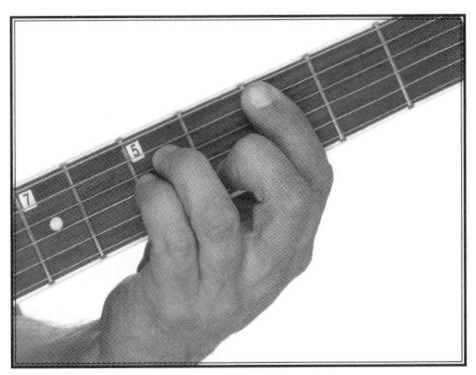

Cm

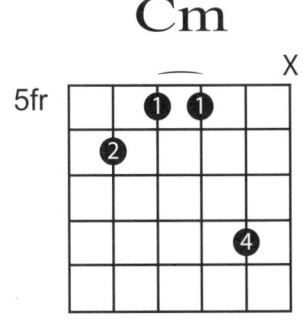
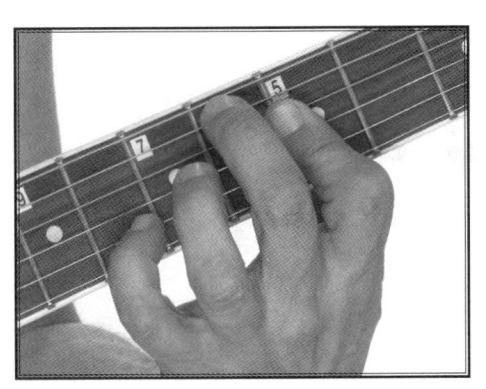

Cm

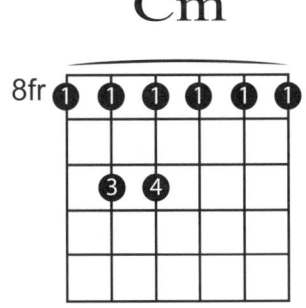
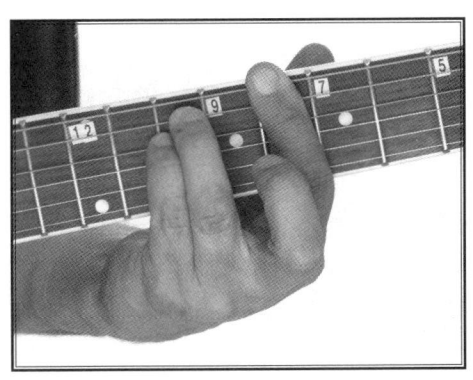

Cm

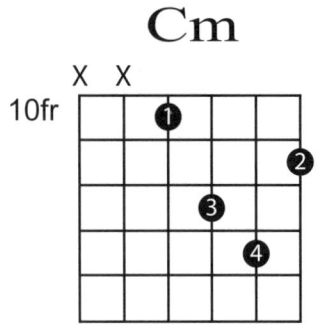

Cm⁶

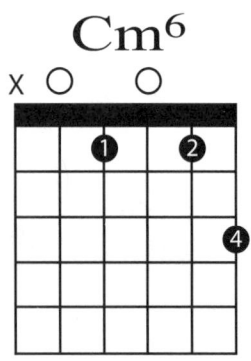

Cm⁶

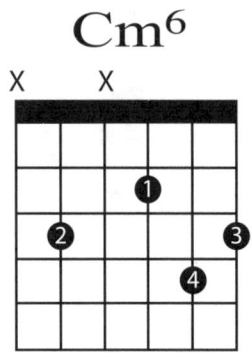

Cm⁶

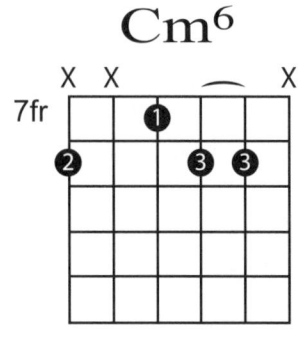

Cm⁷

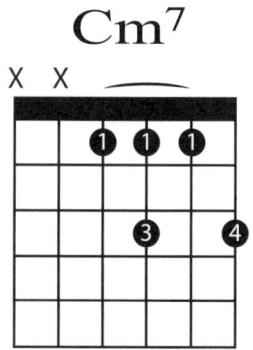  

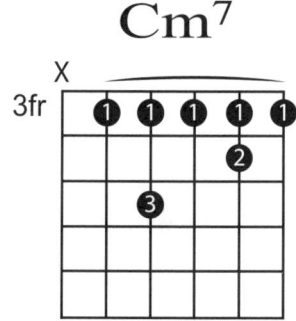 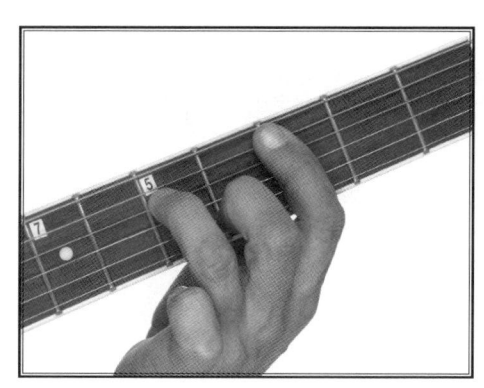 

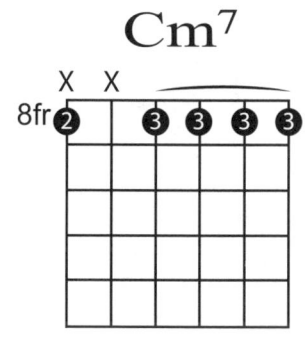 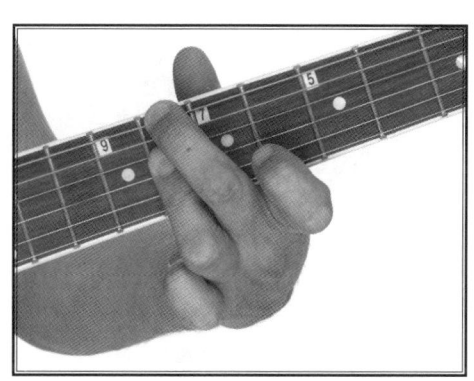 

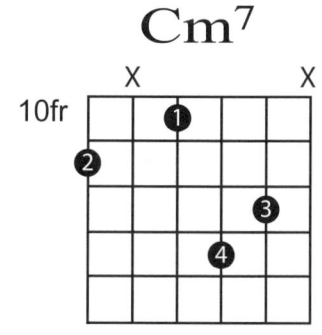  

Cm9

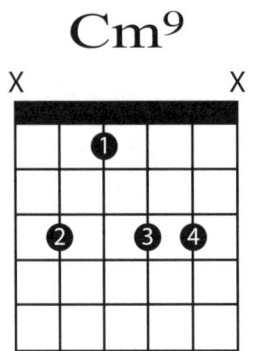  

Cm9

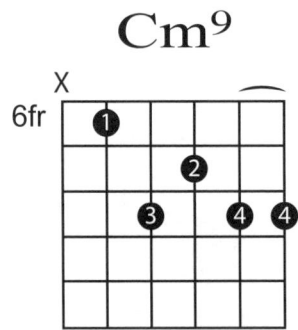  

Cm11

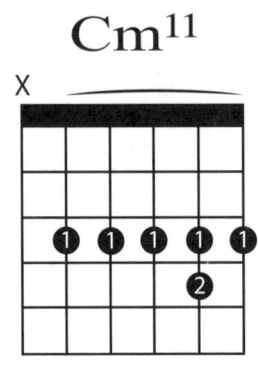 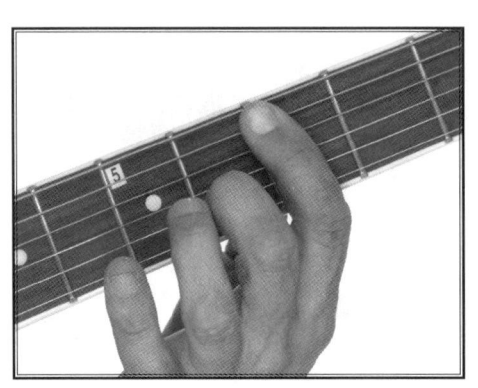 

Cm11

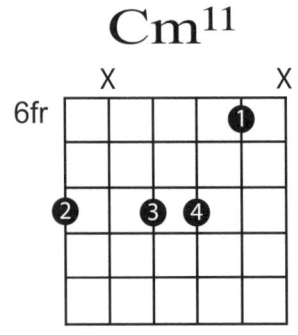  

Cm¹³

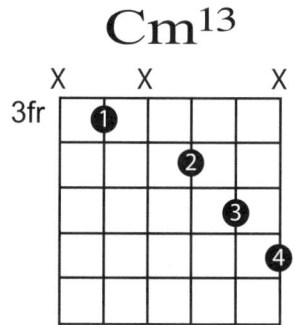  

Cm¹³

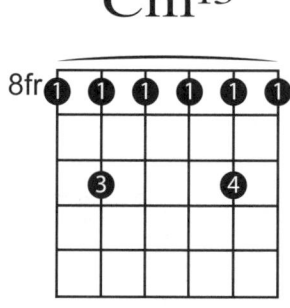  

Cm7♭5

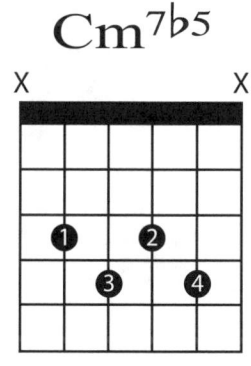  

Cm7♭5

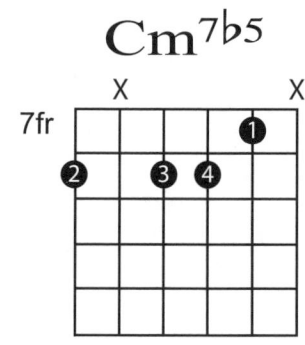  

Cm7b5

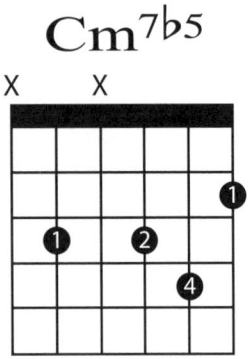

Cm7b5

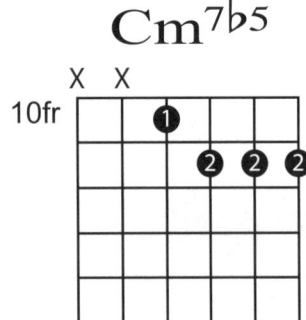

Cm7b5

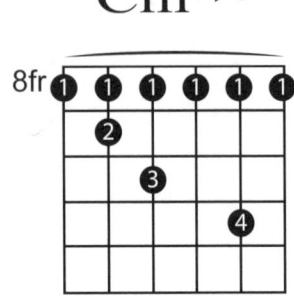

C°7

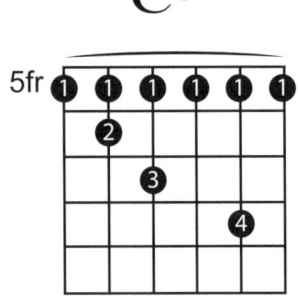

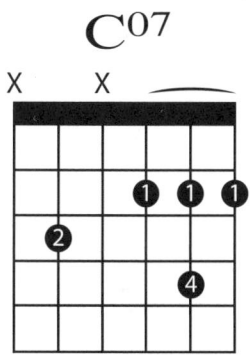  

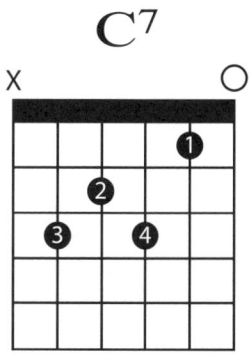  

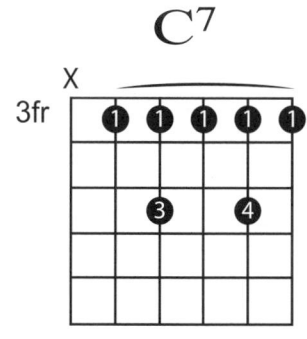  

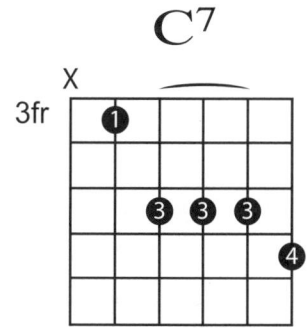 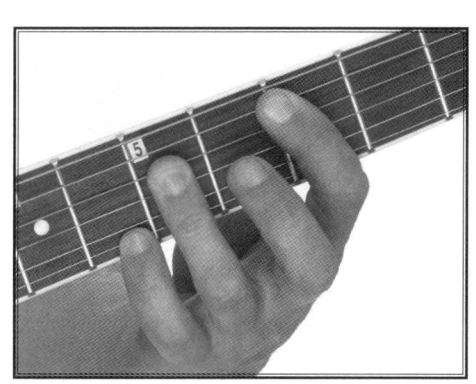 

C7

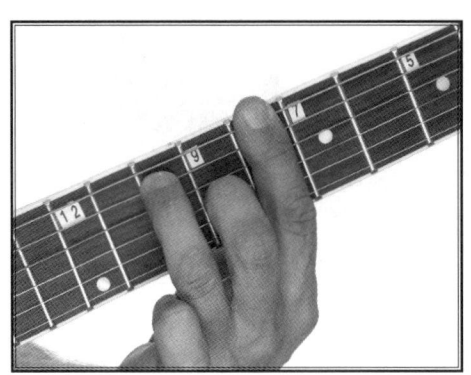

C7

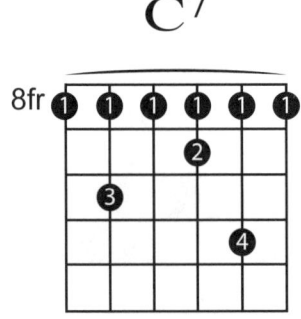

C7

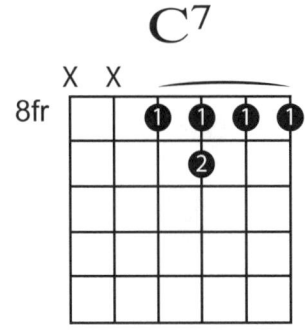

C7sus4

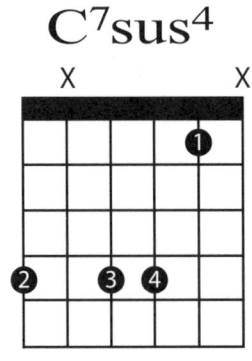

C7sus4

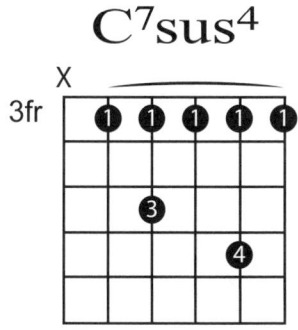
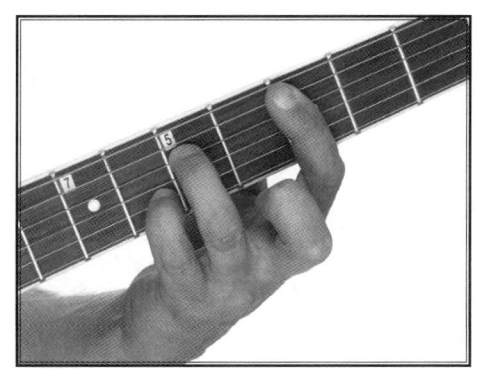

C7♭5

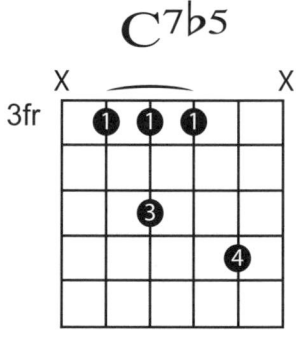

C7♭5

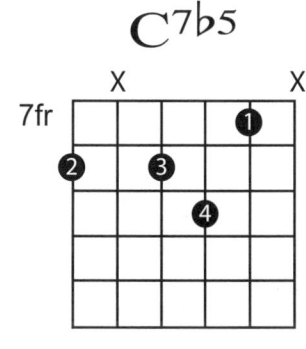

C9

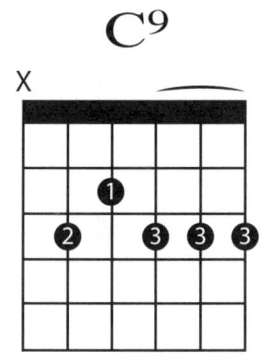

C⁹

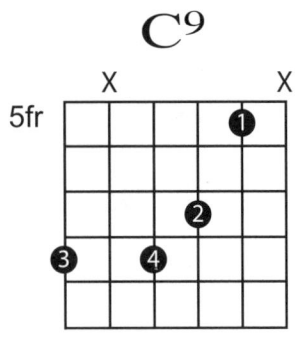
5fr

C⁹

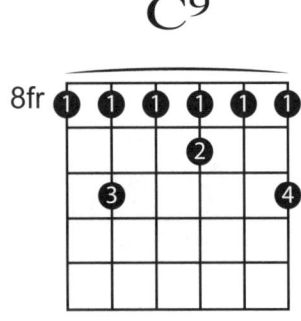
8fr

C⁹sus⁴

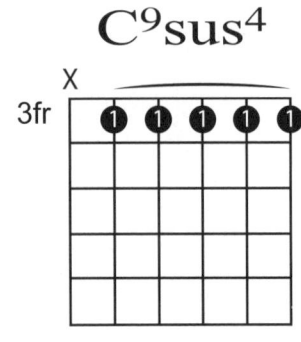
3fr

C⁹sus⁴

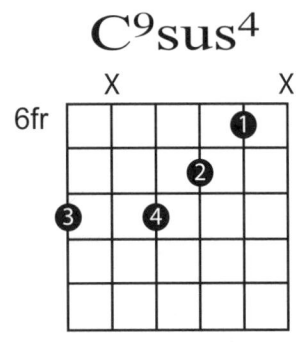
6fr

C^{13}

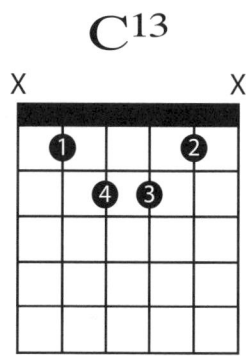  

C^{13}

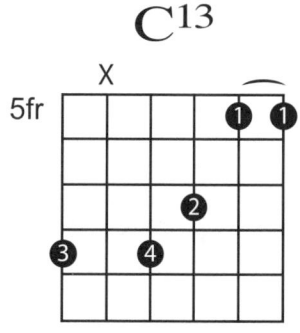  

C^{13}

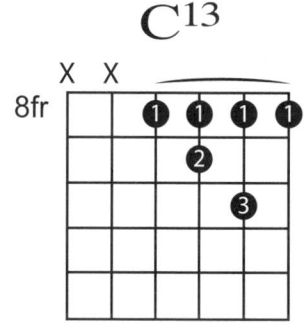 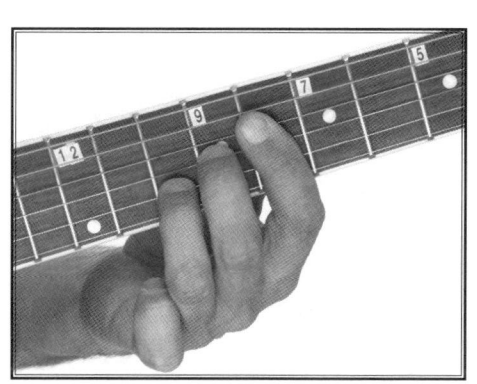 

C^{13}

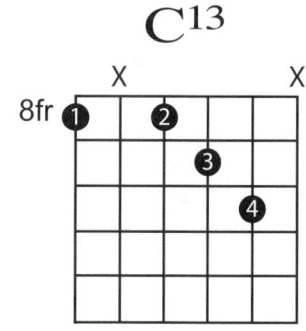  

C+

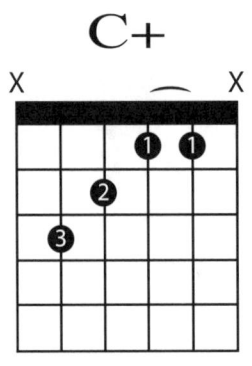  

C+

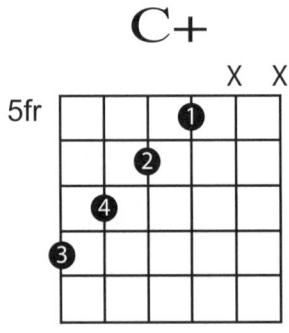  

C5

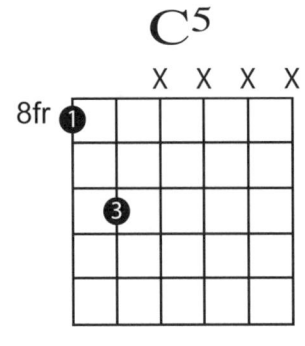 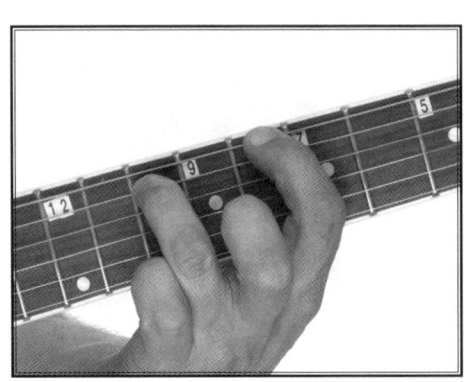 

C5

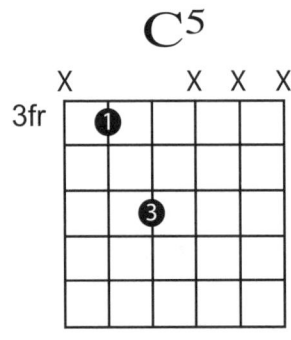 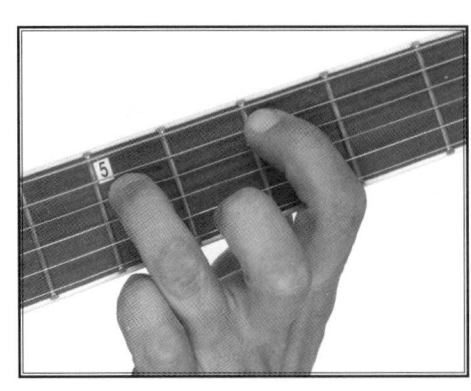 

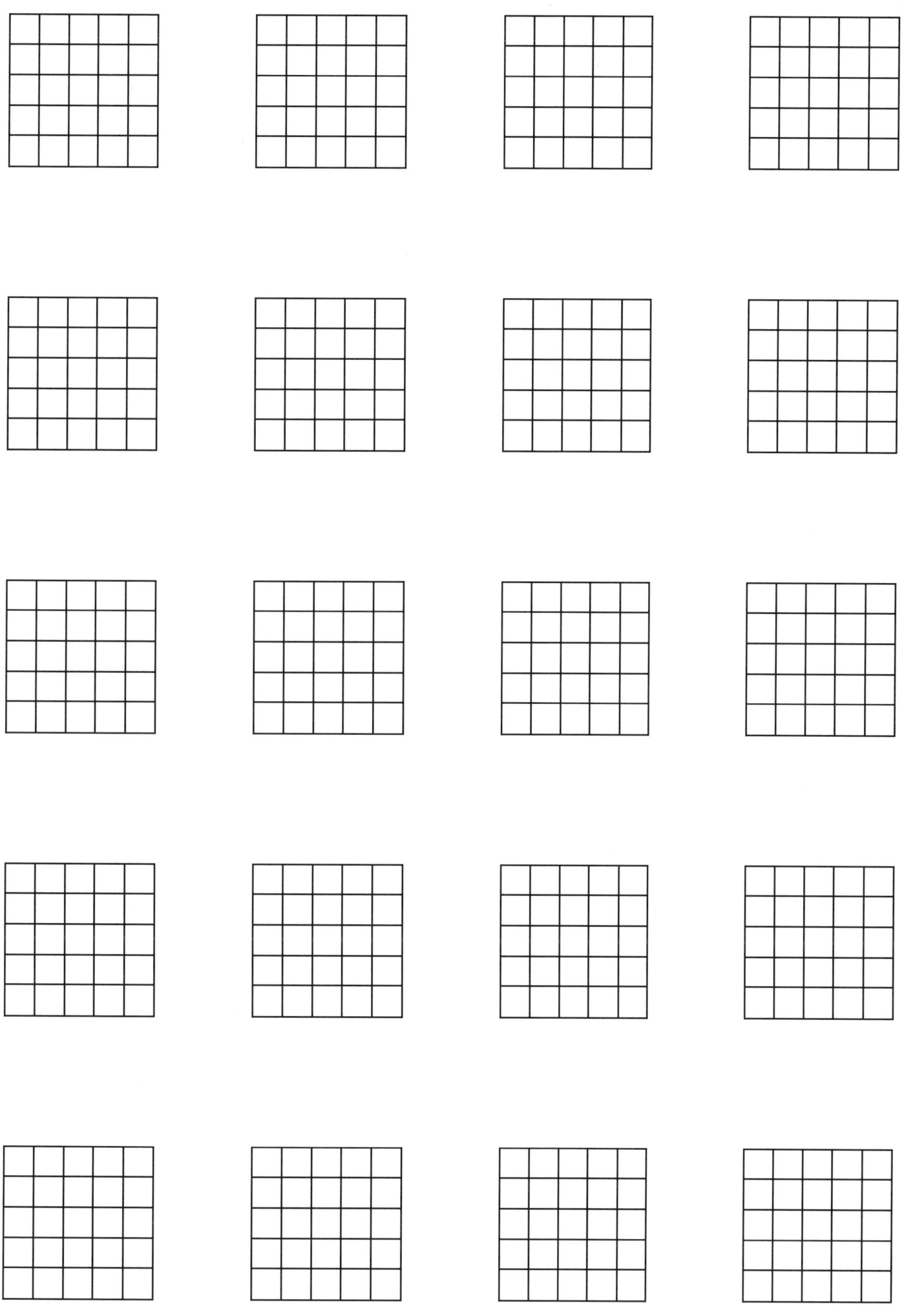

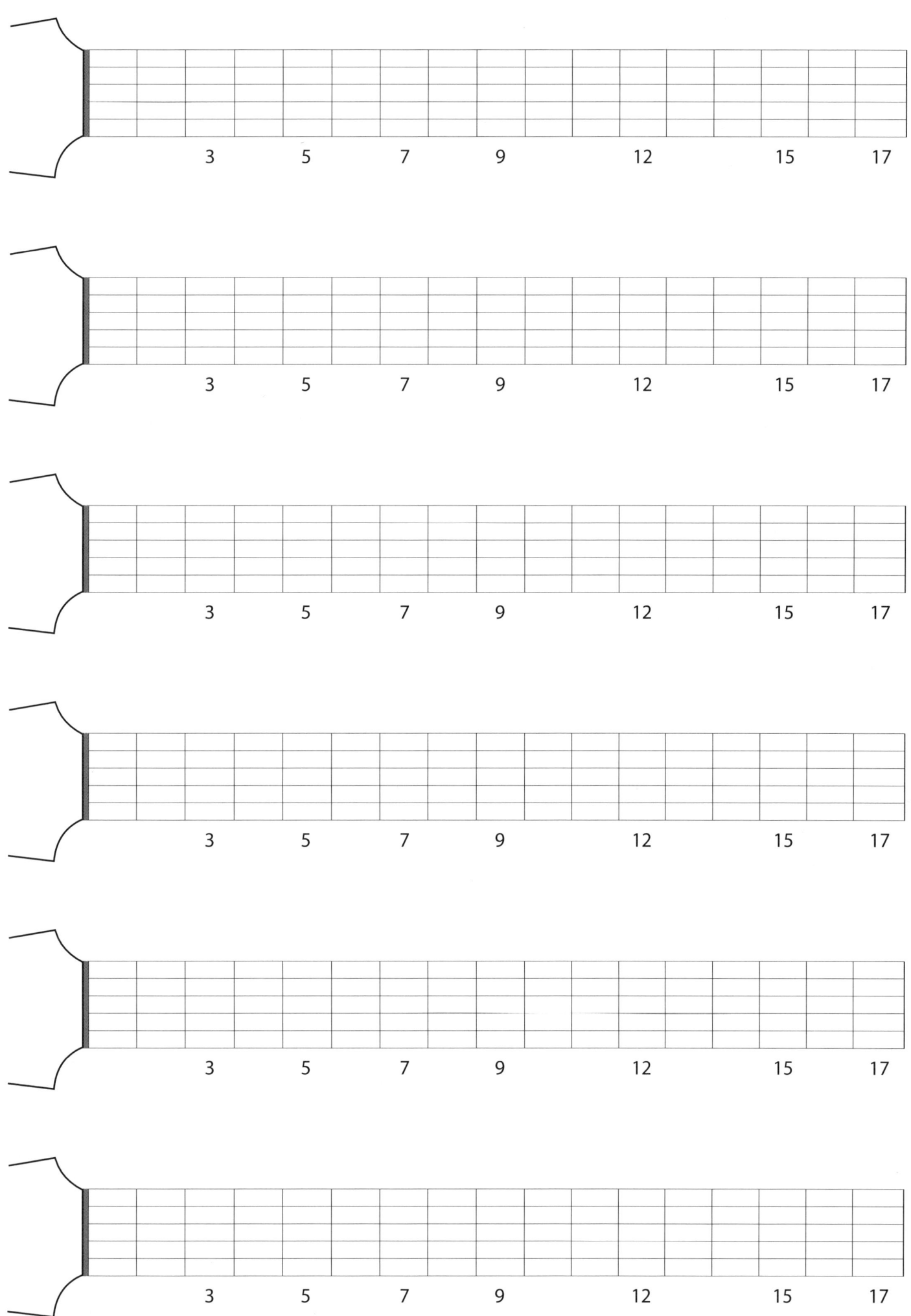

About the Author

John McCarthy
Creator of
The Rock House Method

John is the creator of The Rock House Method®, the world's leading musical instruction system. Over his 30 plus year career, he has written, produced and/or appeared in more than 100 instructional products. Millions of people around the world have learned to play music using John's easy-to-follow, accelerated programs.

John is a virtuoso musician who has worked with some of the industry's most legendary entertainers. He has the ability to break down, teach and communicate music in a manner that motivates and inspires others to achieve their dreams of playing an instrument.

As a musician and songwriter, John blends together a unique style of rock, metal, funk and blues in a collage of melodic compositions. Throughout his career, John has recorded and performed with renowned musicians including Doug Wimbish (Joe Satriani, Living Colour, The Rolling Stones, Madonna, Annie Lennox), Grammy Winner Leo Nocentelli, Rock & Roll Hall of Fame inductees Bernie Worrell and Jerome "Big Foot" Brailey, Freekbass, Gary Hoey, Bobby Kimball, David Ellefson (founding member of seven time Grammy nominee Megadeth), Will Calhoun (B.B. King, Mick Jagger and Paul Simon), Gus G of Ozzy and many more.

To get more information about John McCarthy, his music and his instructional products visit RockHouseSchool.com.